CARS

OF THE WORLD
IN COLOR

by J. D. SCHEEL

Translated by D. Cook-Radmore

Illustrated by Verner Hancke

NEW YORK
E. P. DUTTON & CO., INC.
1967

CARS OF THE WORLD
IN COLOR

Bob Bashforth
12-25-70
FROM BRUCE

FOREWORD

OF ALL THE technical achievements of the pre-atomic age, the *internal combustion engine* remains the most revolutionary in its social consequences. It made possible the creation of the automobile and the motorcycle and made engine power our personal servant. The car is our weekday beast of burden and our seven-league holiday boots.

New and old cars alike may be looked at from a technical, economic, sociological, or legal viewpoint—or just looked at. They may be the subject of critical analysis or passionate interest, or may simply be accepted as a necessity; but the automobile cannot be ignored, for it has become ingrained in our present way of life.

This book tries to survey the main stages in the development of the car. More specialized studies lie outside its scope, as the yardstick was Fame. The choice may seem arbitrary, but now and again the odd ones achieved fame, while others attained wide currency without becoming famous.

The following pages show some of the more outstanding among the 4,000 or more marques which have, over the years, traveled the highways of the world. In this way the author and the illustrator attempt to repay a long-standing debt of gratitude, a debt incurred behind the wheel, in workshops, garages, museums, factories, and drawing offices—and during unforgettable hours spent in and with cars.

A special word of sincere gratitude is due to the public museums, private collectors, clubs, and enthusiasts all over the world who have freely given their help and advice. Likewise, we owe our thanks to the editors and staff of *The Autocar, The Motor, Motor Sport, Automobil Revue, and Skandinavisk Motor Journal,* whose work is the foundation for any inquiry into the automobile and all its ways.

The printers and publishers have given invaluable, constructive advice in the preparation of the book, and have shown superhuman understanding coupled with boundless patience.

It was, therefore, a labor of love to prepare this book which is dedicated, in very deep and sincere respect for the pioneers, to all motorists who still find enjoyment in just driving a car.

J. D. SCHEEL   V. HANCKE

CONTENTS

The colored illustrations of cars are grouped under the countries of manufacture; these are listed alphabetically by their international registration letters, which were established by the 1926 and 1949 International Conventions.

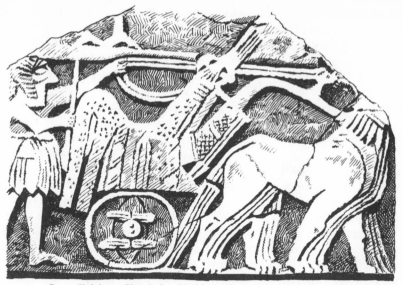

Bas relief from Ur of the Chaldees, depicting a primitive wheel

THE way of the automobile through history can be followed from man's earliest visions of a carriage able to move of its own accord, through the first rudimentary designs, and on to the modern automobile of today. Some 6,000 years were needed to cover the first part of this road, and only a bare hundred years to bring the basic concepts and pioneering efforts to full maturity.

The idea of a vehicle that would move without the muscular aid of man or beast is hardly more recent than the wheel itself, the discovery of which is lost in the earliest days of the history of civilization. It is not even known with any certainty when this most inspired of all man's inventions was made, but an illustration of a wheel has been found in the Sindh Province of India dating from about 4,000 B.C.

The wheel was one of the fundamental factors in material civilization and formed a favorite subject for artists who, in word and picture, created wondrous visions of carriages which could run without a team to pull them. Such notions of a self-propelled vehicle —an *auto-mobile*—persisted in myth and legend through thousands of years of changing civilizations until the day arrived for man's mechanical inventions to be harnessed to the wheel.

Fiery chariots occur in a number of Oriental legends, and reports of such vehicles can be traced back eastward along the caravan routes which linked the Western world to China. From two mysterious empires, "Cathay" to the north and "T'chin" to the south, came travelers' tales of strange happenings including stories of a carriage which moved of its own accord with the aid of fire.

Merchants continued to bring back stories from abroad, and the scholarly English monk *Roger Bacon* (1214-84)

7

wrote "we will be able to construct machines which will propel ships faster than a whole garrison of rowers and which will need only one pilot to guide them. We will be able to move carriages with incredible speed without the assistance of any animal. And we will be able to make machines which, by means of wings, will enable us to fly like birds."

In 1513 Portuguese seafarers reached the coast of China. They were followed by Catholic missionaries, who gained a foothold with the work of Matteo Ricci during the years 1583–1610. Apart from bringing their religion, the missionaries used European medicine and mechanical skills, particularly clockmaking, in order to make contacts with the ruling powers. Ricci's successors, too, had a great insight into technical matters, and one of them, the Jesuit Father *Ferdinand Verbiest*, who worked in China from 1659 until his death in 1688, left a description of a model steam car which he built about 1665–80.

According to his description the little car was two feet long, was built of wood, and "moved easily on four wheels." In the center of this chassis Father Verbiest placed "a small container filled with burning coal," under a metal retort. "Upon the axle for the front wheels I fixed a metal gearwheel, with horizontal teeth across; these engaged in another gearwheel on a vertical shaft and, when the latter turned, it drove the car. This shaft I now fixed into another horizontal wheel, one foot in diameter, around the rim of which I placed in pairs a number of small bars protruding like wings.

"The air [i.e. the steam] which is-

sued with great force from the nozzle of the retort, struck the wings and turned the whole wheel around, thus moving the car. It would now run at a not inconsiderable speed for an hour or more."

Father Verbiest provided steering for his car by fixing a small rod to the rear axle. This could be moved in any direction, and "in the forked end I placed an axle carrying a large wheel, which again was free to rotate. If I now moved the rod obliquely to right or left and fixed it in that position with a screw, the car—driven forward by the power of the steam—continued to run in a larger or smaller circle."

This description is translated from Verbiest's work *Astronomia Europæa,* which appeared in Latin in 1687 after an earlier Chinese edition.

Father Verbiest's steam car certainly merits the title of "automobile," but the question remains whether he built it entirely from his own inspiration. Considering the spreading knowledge of the mechanical uses of steam power in Europe—Giovanni Branca, among others, published a description of a steam turbine in 1629—it is not impossible, although far from certain. There is some reason for suggesting that Father Verbiest, who had won great trust from the Emperor Khang-hi and was in charge of the Imperial Observatory, may have found in the Emperor's library an earlier description of a "fire cart," like those which might have given rise to the old legends.

A steam cart is said to have been mentioned in ancient Chinese writings dating from the Chu dynasty (1125–255 B.C.), and bearing in mind the fact that the Chinese already knew the

Sketch below of Father Verbiest's model steam cart, based on his own description (right)

Astronomia Europaa. Cap. XXIV. 87

Sub finem anni superioris P. Philippus Grimaldi tentavit aliud hydraulicum modo simplicissimo, cujus similitudinem aliquam videre potes in horologio hydraulico, ex ærario P. Marii Bettini edito cum appendice P. Francisci Eschinardi, sed P. Philippus non utitur aquâ, sed tantùm adhibet argentum vivum, & hunc modum ita excoluit, ut planè novum inventum dici possit. Experientiis verò per 7 8. menses captis spes magna affulget, fore, ut hoc horologium superiora omnia certitudine & constantiâ longè superet. Usquemodo necdum obtulit illud Imperatori, jam præparatus offerendum.

CAPUT XXIV.
Pneumatica.

JAm à tribus annis, dum æolipilæ vires examinarem, curriculum bipedalis longitudinis ex levi ligno conficiendum curavi, quatuor rotis facillimè mobilem, in cujus medio vasculum vivis carbonibus plenû, & vasculo æolipilæ imposui; axi priorum rotarm inserui orbem æneum dentatum, dentibus transversim extantibus, & ad horizontem parallelis, quibus apprehensis per aliam rotulam, insertam axi perpendiculari ad horizontem, axe illo circumeunte currus movebatur. Hunc autem axem inserui alteri rotæ ad horizontem parallelæ, cujus diameter erat unius pedis, & in convexa hujus rotæ curvatura circumcirca apposui binos asserculos, tamquam alas extantes, quas ventus, per tubulum angustum æolipilæ violenter expulsus, impellens celerrimo motu totam hanc rotam circumagebat, & pariter currum impellebat, qui per unam horam, & ampliùs (quanto scilicet tempore durabat ventus ex æolipila violenter expulsus) in motu non adeo lento poterat perseverare: ne igitur

88 *Astronomia Europaa. Cap. XXIV.*

tur spatium à curriculo conficiendum nimis in longum excurreret, axi medio posteriorum rotarum apposui temonem, in omnem partem facilè flexibilem, & temonis extremo bifurcato inserui axem; ipsum denique axem inserui rotæ majoris diametri, facillimè etiam mobilem. Itaque temone ad dextram vel lævam obliquè inflexo, atque in illo situ per cochleam firmato, curriculus æolipilæ vento impulsus, perpetuum ferebatur in circulum, magnum vel parvum, pro atrij sive aulæ, in qua movebatur, amplitudine, prout scilicet temo magis vel minùs obliquè inflectebatur. Atque hæc quidem machina est principium motûs, quem scilicet facilè communicare poteram cuilibet alteri machinæ currui imposîtæ, exempli gratiâ naviculæ papyraceæ, quæ velis suis, tamquam vento turgidis instructa, semper in gyrum circumambularet, qualem obtuli fratri majori Imperatoris, totum artis opus ipsa machina occultante, & deforis aditu duntaxat venti æolipilâ expulsi strepitu, instar venti scilicet venti, aut aquarum circùm navim frementium. Subinde etiam per alium tubulum æolipilæ ferruminatum venti erumpentis vim divisi, cujus tubuli extremo, in modum fistulæ præparato, philomelæ modulantis cantum perfectè referebam. Subinde etiam præludium campanulæ horologij hoc instrumento in cantilenas suas animavi: dato hoc principio motûs, multa alia non injucunda excogitare, facile est.

CAPUT XXV.
Musica.

EOdem illo tempore, quo P. Philippus Grimaldi machinam illam hydraulicam, de qua suprà, Imperatori obtulit, P. Thomas Pereyra Lusitanus, qui jam à 6. circiter annis

ab

power of steam by 800 B.C., and the wheel earlier still, it cannot be completely discounted that a Chinese steam cart may have inspired the early poetic descriptions and later prophecies by European thinkers.

Father Verbiest's construction, or reconstruction, of a model automobile using a steam turbine found no direct descendant in Europe, although during the time of the Greeks the idea had occupied the minds of men and the power of steam had begun to be realized.

Plato was aware of steam power, and *Hero of Alexandria* listed, about 150 B.C., some seventy inventions making use of steam; these included the "aeolipile," a wind (or rather, steam) sphere, but none aimed at a self-propelled vehicle.

After the days of the Roman empire the pages of history are blank so far as steam power is concerned, and until the sixteenth and seventeenth centuries no attempts at harnessing it to mechanical ends are chronicled. The so-called "automobiles" of the Roman Emperors may be ignored, since slaves or animals were concealed inside them. Nor was the battle chariot designed about A.D. 1500 by *Leonardo da Vinci* a genuine automobile, as it was moved by human effort. A project for a mechanically propelled vehicle has been attributed to *Sir Isaac Newton,* but this is due to a misinterpretation of Newton's works.

Various—more or less historically authenticated—wind-driven vehicles cannot really be regarded as automobiles, which must by definition have a mechanical means of propulsion, and the honor of having built the first mechanically propelled vehicle capable of carrying goods and passengers belongs to the French artillery officer, *Nicolas Joseph Cugnot,* who constructed and drove a steam tractor in Paris in the year 1769.

Cugnot's memorable design had first been executed as a scale model in 1763, and a full-sized version was built six years later; in 1770 he drove the vehicle in the presence of the Duke of Choiseul at a speed approaching 2½ mph. The exact dimensions of Cugnot's first tractor are no longer known—it overturned and was then broken up—but the idea was not abandoned. In 1771, after some eighteen months of work, a new and larger tractor was ready. This was to carry a load of four or five tons, and the test run was eagerly awaited; but even in those far-off days French internal politics were so involved that a change of government took place, with unforeseen consequences.

The Duke of Choiseul, who had made a grant of 20,000 livres for the construction of Cugnot's vehicle, ceased to be a minister. His successor felt his ministerial seat so insecure that he dared not give the army even the modest means for buying fuel and paying two days' labor by two men. As a result, Cugnot's tractor was allowed to remain in the arsenal until, thirty years later, it was rescued from oblivion in February 1800 and moved into the *Conservatoire Nationale des Arts et Métiers.* There it stands today in all its glory, its massive iron-shod wheels towering above a tall man's head. Although it never ran, it is the oldest automobile in the world. The enormous three-wheeled carriage is built of heavy timber beams, and an almost

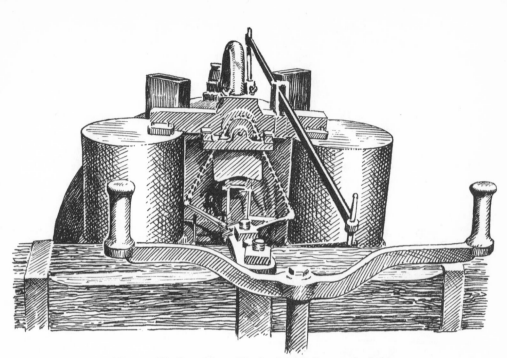

The world's first driver, Nicolas Joseph Cugnot, had this impressive sight from his driving seat

spherical copper boiler with a built-in furnace is located over the front wheel which is driven by two single-acting pistons.

At about the same time a pupil of *James Watt* named *William Murdock* was experimenting in England with a steam locomotive, but he got no farther than producing a small model; this was tried out on the public roads at dead of night, and nearly frightened the life out of God-fearing folk.

In 1801 *Robert Trevithick* built a steam road locomotive which was capable of carrying four passengers up quite steep gradients. It caught fire, however, and was replaced in 1803 by an improved version. By now encouraging results were being achieved in both Europe and America, and around 1820 developments really began to get under way.

Onésiphore Pecqueur, in France, built a steam carriage in 1828 which was fitted with a differential on the rear axle and had steering of similar design to that used today. He was, however, so far ahead of his time that he died in penury.

At the same time *Goldsworthy Gurney* and *Walter Hancock* in England started to construct really roadworthy steam carriages, and made attempts to use steam transport as a commercial proposition. Hancock's *Infant* was probably the world's first taxicab, and he used *Era, Enterprise, Sun,* and *Automaton* to operate a bus service in London. Hancock also built a small, light steam car for private use, and among

Trevithick, 1803

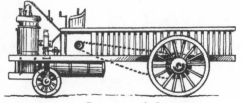

Pecqueur, 1828

Hancock, 1833–34

Bollée's "L'Obéissante," 1873

others who followed his example were the *Marquis of Stafford,* who used a steamer made to his order by Thomas Rickett, the *Tangye* brothers, and, in France, *Amedée Bollée père* who constructed a number of admirable buses and carriages at Le Mans in the 1870s.

One of the problems connected with steam vehicles was that of stoking the boiler. The fireman, or "chauffeur," had a thankless and difficult task, and this led many designers to toy with the idea of using liquid fuel in place of coal. It is not certain who introduced this major improvement; according to some sources the honor goes to *Joseph Wilkinson,* but it is generally accepted that a Frenchman named *Joseph Ravel* built the first steam car to use liquid fuel in 1868.

While the development of the steam carriage was being energetically pushed ahead, a number of inventors were pursuing their own paths of investigation. *Isaac de Rivaz,* in Switzerland, propelled a carriage in the spring of 1804 by exploding a mixture of hydrogen and air inside a cylinder. In doing this he was perfecting the crude "engine" made by the Dutchman *Chr. Huygens* in 1673, and also basing his design on the Volta pistol which was charged with a mixture of hydrogen and air and ignited by means of an electric spark. Thirteen years later an English clergyman carried out similar experiments using a mixture of hydrogen, steam, and air, but it was a Frenchman, *Jean Joseph Étienne Lenoir,* who in 1860 took out a patent on a two-stroke internal-combustion engine. This was used in 1862–63 to power what was the world's first automobile, in the accepted sense of the word.

While Lenoir's gas engine was very interesting—among other features it had electric ignition—a very real step forward was made when *Nikolaus August Otto* designed the first practical four-cycle gas engine in Germany in 1876, following a principle already outlined by a Frenchman, *Beau de Rochas,* in 1862. Otto built no cars, but between 1870 and 1890 an Austrian named *Siegfried Markus* constructed and tested two single-cylinder vehicles of his own design using crude gasoline engines. Had Markus followed up his farsighted ideas he would have become the father of the modern automobile; as it is, it is now difficult to bestow this honor on any single inventor.

In 1883–84 *Delamare-Deboutteville* built a two-cylinder motor car, and at the Stanley Cycle Show held in London in 1884 a marveling public was able to examine a colored drawing of *Edward Butler's* motor-driven tricycle with a twin-cylinder engine, fitted with electrical ignition and a carburetor of quite modern design. But these beginnings were not followed up either.

A turning point was reached in 1885 with the independent experiments of *Karl Benz* and *Gottlieb Daimler,* in Germany. Though they lived not far from each other, at Mannheim and Cannstatt respectively, there was no liaison between the two pioneers. Benz's first road vehicle was a three-wheeler, while Daimler started with a motorcycle fitted with two extra stabilizer wheels. Both had four-cycle motors, Benz's previous experiments with units of the two-cycle type having proved unsuccessful. Everything was set for Germany to become the cradle of the automobile.

Daimler was mainly a motor engineer, and had worked for ten years in the *Gasmotorenfabrik Deutz AG* at Cologne, a factory controlled by N. A. Otto and Eugen Langen. There was a

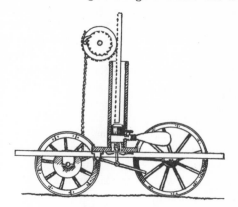

de Rivaz, 1804

Lenoir, 1862

Delamare-Deboutteville, 1884

certain amount of friction with his colleagues, and Daimler left the firm at the beginning of 1881.

Otto's and Daimler's paths did not cross again, and France, not Germany, became the nursery of the automobile, when Daimler's patent rights for that country were bought by *Édouard Sarazin* for the firm of Perrin, Panhard & Cie in the year 1887. Sarazin died not long after and his widow married *Émile Levassor*, who took over the patents and founded the concern of Panhard & Levassor. It was this firm that brought the gasoline automobile into being; their first car left the factory in 1890 and with it the modern automobile was born.

The steam car was still in a strong position, however, and the electric car

Daimler "Sidewheeler," 1885

Benz "Gas engine vehicle," 1886

was a serious competitor. Steam was a thoroughly understood and controllable source of power, while the silence of electricity caught the imagination of a large number of inventors.

When, in 1860, storage batteries replaced the galvanic cells which had been used up till then, the electric car found many partisans on both sides of the Atlantic. It had many advantages to offer—it was almost noiseless, and it was light; but the frequent need for recharging the batteries was a considerable limitation. The gasoline car had come to stay, but it should be noted that an electric car took the first official world speed record in 1898, when the *Marquis de Chasseloup-Laubat* and *Camille Jenatzy* staged their historic duels, gradually stepping up their speeds from 39 mph to just over 65 mph. Nor did the steam car yield pride of place at once to the new designs, and as late as 1906 a *Stanley Steamer* figures in the list of American records with a speed of 127.6 mph.

Developments in both design and industrial manufacture forged ahead during the last decade of the nineteenth century. *Panhard & Levassor* have a valid claim to seniority among automobile manufacturers. The factory built its first car in 1889 and went into regular production in 1891. *René Panhard's* close business connections with the bicycle manufacturer *Armand Peugeot,* who had already built a number of steam cars, brought Peugeot into the still narrow circle of those who made motorcars, and the first Peugeot "quadricycle" was on the roads of France by 1890.

Among the firms which began to manufacture automobiles during the

Jenatzy's "La Jamais Contente," 1899

nineties were *de Dion-Bouton, Renault, Darracq, Berliet* and *Delahaye in* France; *Daimler, Benz* and *Lutzmann* in Germany; the *Daimler Motor Company, Lanchester, Wolseley, Arrol-Johnston, Sunbeam* and *Swift* in Britain; *F.I.A.T.* in Italy; *Miesse, Vivinus* and *Germain* in Belgium; *Martini* in Switzerland; and in several other countries were factories with names that have been forgotten and which never fulfilled the fond hopes of their founders.

While the first European automobile factories were building up a fairly regular sale for their products some five years or so before the turn of the century, progress in the USA was rather hesitant. The idea of the automobile was alive, but the basic problems were far from solved. No one could predict with certainty whether steam, electricity, or the internal combustion engine was best suited to the mechanical propulsion of a carriage. No one could foretell the way in which the road network should be developed, and at that time the American highways were totally unsuited to motorcars. And, besides, the American automobile pioneers knew very little of what was being achieved in Europe.

European road transport was already well organized before the first railway

lines were laid, and this was of incalculable benefit to Europe's first automobile designers. In the United States, on the contrary, the railways preceded the roads, and there were consequently no trunk routes across the country.

As on the European side of the Atlantic, the first car to run in the USA was powered by steam. In 1804–1805 *Oliver Evans* in Chicago built a large amphibious vehicle—the "Arukter Amphibolos"—powered by a steam engine; but like Cugnot's vehicle it had no direct successors. Later *Sylvester H. Roper* of Massachusetts produced a number of steam cars, but before his and other steam designer's ideas managed to gain ascendancy a number of inventors had begun to use the internal combustion engine or electricity.

In 1872 *George B. Brayton* took out his first patent for a primitive two-cycle internal combustion engine, which was used experimentally in a streetcar and a bus. This engine was shown at the centenary exhibition in Philadelphia in 1876, and indirectly came to play a major part in the birth of the American automobile industry. Of more direct significance, however, was the fact that two brothers, *Charles E.* and *J. Frank Duryea,* and *Elwood*

Panhard & Levassor, 1891

Haynes made independent test runs in cars with internal combustion engines which they had built themselves, in September 1893 and July 1894 respectively.

At the same time the electric motor had its keen supporters, including *Thomas A. Edison,* who in particular discovered the possibility of using electric traction for railway locomotives and streetcars, and the first American electric car is ascribed to *William Morrison,* who drove his noiseless wonder around Chicago in 1892.

The problems involved in building satisfactory cars with internal combustion engines or steam engines at first gave the electric motor clear advantages over its competitors. The restricted range of operation between charging of the batteries was no great disadvantage so long as the car could be used only in built-up areas, and on trunk roads automobiles were unable to cover large distances whatever their means of propulsion. The restrictions brought about by these difficulties were to a very great extent to decide the design of the early American cars and the structure of the industry.

The early automobile manufacturers in the USA concentrated on very light cars, the production of which was na-

Oliver Evans, 1805

turally suited to the bicycle manufacturers with the necessary machinery and a good deal of the basic technical know-how. A number of the American industrialists pioneering the automobile had had their early technical and business training in cycle factories, including the Duryea brothers from the very beginning and *William S. Knudsen* from the era of the industrial expansion.

The horse-drawn carriage manufacturers, who flourished in the USA of those days, formed the other point of departure for the American automobile industry. The *Studebaker* concern, for instance, can trace its beginnings back directly to the days of horse carriages, when the five Studebaker brothers set up *The Studebaker Brothers Manufacturing Company* in 1852. Another of the great names in the carriage-making business, *William Crapo Durant,* took his place in the history of the automobile when he founded *General Motors.*

While the European automobile industry's pattern of development was that of hand-made vehicles produced by individual designers, the building of automobiles in the USA had an industrial look about it from the start. It was because of economic developments in the bicycle industry that the American automobile became an industrial factory-made product from the outset. A fall-off in the market for bicycles more or less forced the leading manufacturers and their component suppliers to make motorcars, and to make them in large numbers at a low price.

The first attempt to set up an American car industry was made by *The Pope Manufacturing Company* in

Duryea, 1893

Haynes, 1894

Hartford, Connecticut. This firm was the largest manufacturer of bicycles in the USA around 1890, and when the market for cycles began to drop the management became interested in exploiting the possibilities which the automobile seemed to offer. An approach was made to *Hiram P. Maxim* (better remembered today as the designer of a machine-gun silencer) to try out the tricycle fitted with an internal combustion engine which he had designed in 1895. Maxim's design met with no great enthusiasm from the Pope Company. The founder of the firm, *Colonel Albert A. Pope,* main-

tained that "people wouldn't want to sit on top of an explosion," and for this reason the factory started on the manufacture of an electric car known as the *Columbia*. It met with success, but this very success brought about the end of Pope's first venture into the automobile-making business.

This paradox may be explained by the interest shown by the forces of American capital in building up vast concerns. The *Motor Carriage Department* of the Pope factory was bought up in 1899 by *The Electric Vehicle Company,* which sought a monopoly of both car manufacture and taxi operation over the whole of the United States, gambling on the dominance of the electric motor over the steam and internal combustion engines. When this technical gamble failed, the financial maneuvers failed too; by 1907 the Electric Vehicle Company was ruined. Ironically, the sole asset found during the bankruptcy proceedings was an all-embracing patent on mechanical vehicles with internal combustion engines.

Patent No. 549,160 played a singular role in the history of the automobile in the United States. It was granted on November 5, 1895, to *George Baldwin Selden,* and modestly covered the entire design, down to the smallest detail, of carriages with internal combustion engines. The reason why Selden was able to claim protection for his invention several years after other American inventors had built and run cars using internal combustion motors was the fact that his original application had been filed in 1879. The actual grant of the patent was, however, delayed for sixteen years because he made constant changes in his specification.

Selden practiced as a patent attorney in order to be able to combine his hobby of engineering with his livelihood, and when he saw Brayton's engine exhibited in Philadelphia it gave him the necessary inspiration to produce a vastly improved two-cycle engine. Starting from this he worked out a plan for a road engine, incorporating all the features of design which would go into a carriage using an internal combustion motor. At this stage he filed his patent application, and then started looking for the capital needed to turn his design into a reality.

While Selden was searching in vain for financial support for his design, a large number of designers were steadily working on carriages with internal combustion motors in complete ignorance of the dormant patent application and the patent which was, at long last, issued. The Duryea brothers, Haynes, and Maxim were followed in March 1896 by *Charles Brady King* and in June of the same year by *Henry Ford.*

The patent expert of the Pope factory was, however, aware of Selden's patent, and he had advised that the firm should cease production of carriages with gasoline motors. This was no great sacrifice, since the main production line was in any case electric cars. But in the course of the negotiations for the Electric Vehicle Company's takeover of the Pope factory, patent problems arose again, and in order to remove any obstacle to their grandiose plans for the domination of the USA automobile industry, the Electric Vehicle Company bought out Selden's patent for $10,000 and one fifth of any profits the patent might bring in.

In view of the all-embracing nature of the patent the price was a low one; but Selden was probably modest in his demands, since up till then he had made no profit from his invention, and the Electric Vehicle Company was convinced, in any case, that the electric motor was superior to the gasoline engine. The company probably saw the possession of the patent as a sort of insurance, and when the electric motor gamble brought the firm into difficulties it seemed that this policy was going to pay off. With the Selden patent in its possession the tottering concern was in fact able to demand that all the companies established in the meantime for the manufacture of carriages with internal combustion engines either cease production or pay royalties.

This was a most uncomfortable surprise for the new industry and the manufacturers concerned put up a spirited fight. In a test case brought against the biggest firm, *The Winton Motor Carriage Company,* judgment was, however, given in favor of the

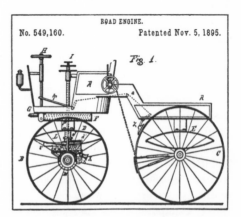

ROAD ENGINE.
No. 549,160.   Patented Nov. 5, 1895.

Fig. 1.

G. B. Selden's all-embracing patent

patent holders. After this the industry was ready to come to terms, and in 1903 an *Association of Licensed Automobile Manufacturers* was set up, which made a levy of 1¼ per cent of the catalogue price of every car produced. This royalty was split in the proportion of one fifth to Selden, two fifths to the Electric Vehicle Company, and the remaining two fifths to the newly created association, which rapidly became the main organization for the entire industry.

The year after its formation it had thirty members, and its prime interest soon became a fight against those firms which remained outside the association. This was partly from a desire for a "closed shop," but partly also from more altruistic motives—for many of the so-called manufacturers of automobiles produced and sold vehicles of very doubtful quality.

With the utmost delicacy the established and organized automobile factories took care to draw a veil of forgetfulness over their own origins. The companies named so far stemmed from the existing cycle or carriage industry, apart from Ford who began as an automobile manufacturer and remained outside the association. David Buick began in the plumbing business and came to cars after having dealt in stationary and marine engines. *Harry A. Knox* was initially in a firm making electrical machinery. The *Stanley* brothers, who made steam cars, started with violins and photographic plates. *James Ward Packard* was a manufacturer of electric cables and similar products, and *George N. Pierce*, later to become the father of the famous *Pierce-Arrow* car, started his career as a manu-

King, 1896

Ford, 1896

facturer of birdcages and refrigerators, changed to bicycles, and later moved on to motorcars.

The inevitable outcome of the "patent manufacturers" association was the birth in 1905 of a rival organization with the title of the *American Motor Car Manufacturers Association,* which under the leadership of Henry Ford went into battle against the Selden patent. This organization, too, listed important firms among its members: *Reo,* which was started in 1904 by *Ransom Eli Olds,* who had founded the Olds Motor Vehicle Company in 1897 (later the Olds Motor Works), builders of the famous single-cylinder Curved Dash Runabout; *Marmon,* founded by *Howard C. Marmon,* who started out by making mill machinery; and *Maxwell-Briscoe,* which was established in 1903

Knox, 1901

by an engineer, *Jonathan D. Maxwell* and a businessman, *Benjamin Briscoe,* who had taken an interest in Buick and who in 1910 tried to organize a big group in opposition to General Motors.

The association of "patentless" manufacturers lost their lawsuit in 1909, and was disbanded. Henry Ford, however, refused to give up and after a long and expensive case he won his appeal in 1911. This caused the "patent manufacturers" organization to break up, and the Electric Vehicle Company's last hope of being a dominant factor in the American automobile industry was lost.

During the lawsuit a Selden car was built according to the patent specification. It ran, although not very convincingly. The court of appeal found the patent valid only for cars using Selden's improved version of the Brayton two-cycle engine, and as all American manufacturers used four-cycle engines the industry was at long last set free from restrictions.

Brayton's engine bows out of the story here, having played a menacing role in the wings for thirty-five years— but even now there is still one result of the doings of Brayton and Selden: through various reorganizations the

"patent" association became the *Automobile Manufacturers Association,* which today embraces the whole of the American automobile industry.

In Britain the birth of the motor-car industry was delayed by archaic legislation. The Locomotive Act of 1867 not only imposed a speed limit of 4 mph in the country and 2 mph in towns, but required a man on foot carrying a red flag to precede any vehicle on the public highway. In 1878 a further Act disposed of the detested red flag, but it was not until November 1896 that the repeal of these Acts and the raising of the speed limit to 12 mph opened Britain's roads to the automobile age. November 14th of that year, "Emancipation Day," saw a curiously assorted procession of vehicles start out from the Central Hall, Westminster, en route for Brighton. The official results listed ten finishers, led by two Bollée tricars and a Panhard & Levassor "Wagonette." Certainly, for the next few years the bulk of cars on British roads were of Continental origin.

In America the Selden patent dominated the early years; in Britain a would-be monopolist arose in the flamboyant person of *Harry John Lawson.* His unshakable belief in the future of the automobile and his vigorous efforts to popularize it culminated in a fantastic series of financial operations designed to corner the entire British motor manufacturing industry. The foundation in 1895 of the *British Motor Syndicate,* acquiring Continental patent rights, and then the *Great Horseless Carriage Company,* among others, to exploit them in manufacture ended in disaster as a result of incompetent management and financial jugglery. But individual designers were beginning to achieve success around the turn of the century, among them *F. W. Lanchester,* whose efficient and unorthodox designs were years ahead of their time, *Herbert Austin,* then working for the Wolseley Sheep Shearing Company, and *Montague Stanley Napier* who was to use the prestige of his great racing cars to promote his more prosaic touring cars.

As we follow the motorcar on its way from fantasy to reality, it is worth pausing a moment to look at the shape and design of the automobile at the beginning of the twentieth century. From being merely a converted horse-drawn carriage, it had become in just under twenty years a vehicle conceived solely as an automobile. It was only the bonds of tradition which dictated similarities with the horse-drawn carriage, and they have still not been entirely thrown off.

In the motor, transmission, and many other details the basic elements of today were beginning to take shape. The better motorcars of those days had a twin-cylinder motor delivering some 4–8 horsepower, and in a few

Oldsmobile, 1901

cases a four-cylinder engine with twice the power. Gasoline and air were mixed in a primitive surface carburettor. The ignition was by platinum tubes kept red-hot by means of special burners. The inlet valves were opened by the suction in the cylinder as the pistons went down, and only the exhaust valves were actuated by the camshaft. The horsepower so laboriously produced was transferred through a leather-faced cone clutch and a crude, "crash" gearbox to a countershaft driving two chains. These carried what power was left to the rear wheels, which had a rather doubtful grip on the road through solid rubber or iron tires.

Already in 1901, however, the best of the horseless carriages from the nineteenth century were hopelessly out of date. The main design principles of the modern automobile had appeared. Electrical ignition replaced the hot-tube, both sets of valves were opened by camshafts, the early gilled cooling tubes were being replaced by honeycomb radiators, shaft-drive began to be adopted, pneumatic tires appeared on the wheels, and steering with a wheel and gearing took the place of the earlier tiller or clumsy screw mechanism.

The most remarkable aspect of this rapid development was the revival of half-forgotten technical discoveries. Cardan transmission, for instance, is often attributed to *Louis Renault.* He was undoubtedly the first to put a car with a cardan-jointed shaft-drive into series production, but the actual inventor was an Italian, *Girolamo Cardano,* who, we are told on good authority, was stillborn in the year 1501 but was brought to life by being dipped in a dish of warm wine. It must

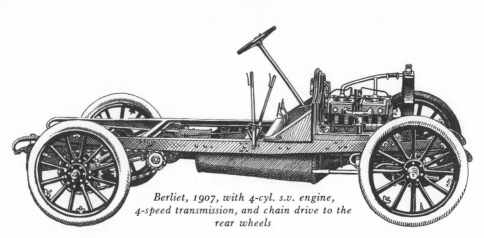

*Berliet, 1907, with 4-cyl. s.v. engine,
4-speed transmission, and chain drive to the
rear wheels*

have been quite an effective remedy, as he lived for many years as a famous doctor and astrologer—and the inventor of the universal joint. The differential was patented in 1827 by Pecqueur, and Walter Hancock in 1831 fitted his steam carriage "Infant I" with as up-to-date a refinement as a limited-slip differential. Rear wheel suspension by means of a De Dion axle, which has two half-shafts for transmitting the power, and an axle tube locating the rear wheels, also dates from the steam car age, and was patented in 1894 by the *de Dion-Bouton* firm.

Both general progress and the revival of inventions that had been ahead of their time were encouraged by motor sport. Speed and reliability contests for cars had been held since 1894, and the first real motor race was held on June 11–13, 1895, from Paris to Bordeaux and back again. Levassor drove a Panhard & Levassor to victory at an average speed of 15½ mph over the 740-mile course, and in so doing sparked off the progress made on the main roads of Europe. Speeds rose as design problems were solved, but no single invention contributed more to the motorcar's con-

quest of the highways and byways of the world than the pneumatic tire patented in 1888 by the Scots veterinary surgeon *John Boyd Dunlop.*

Dunlop's "pneumatic wheel covering" was originally intended only for his son's bicycle, but it was taken up with such enthusiasm by other cyclists that the invention was exploited commercially. However, before he was able to do this, Dunlop had to battle his way through lengthy lawsuits, for an Englishman named *Robert William Thomson* had already patented a different type of pneumatic tire in 1845.

Many of the automative pioneers were extremely skeptical of the idea of "riding on air," but in spite of the doubts the idea gained ground. The first pneumatic tire specifically intended for motorcars was made in 1895 by two brothers, *André* and *Édouard Michelin,* and as it gradually became possible to produce reliable covers the skeptics stopped filling the space intended for air with straw, gelatine, or various other strange substances.

The "air tires," which were first despised by one and all, won the big races on the open road from Paris to

Amsterdam, to Ostend, to Berlin and Vienna. Through choking dust, boiling sunshine, or driving rain the brave drivers forced their towering and heavy cars at speeds which later generations find it hard to believe. Some idea of the nature of these races may be grasped from the fact that the race from Paris to Berlin in 1901 was won at an average speed of 44.5 mph; many a modern motorist would be pleased to match this performance by *Henri Fournier.*

These heroic days came to an abrupt and tragic end with the 1903 Paris–Madrid race when the French government stopped the contest at Bordeaux because of numerous injuries, some fatal, to competitors and spectators. Bordeaux thus became the finishing point for both the first and the last of the classic town-to-town races, and in that last, epic event *Ferdinand Gabriel* drove a 70 hp Mors to victory at the incredible average speed of 65.2 mph.

Substantial changes had to be made, and out of the classic long-distance races and the *Gordon Bennett Cup* series run during the years 1900–1905 as an international contest for a cup put up by the American newspaper magnate James Gordon Bennett, the *Grand Prix de l'Automobile Club de France* was born in 1906. The first of these races provides the next traditional milestone in the history of the motorcar, and at that time nearly all the important features of modern automobile design were in use. The more notable exceptions were the electric self-starter, hydraulic four-wheel brakes, the car radio, the heater, and automatic transmission.

The changes in international motor sport quickly led to alterations in the design and size of the competing cars. The enormous cars with engines of 13–14 liters capacity (796–858 cu. in.) gave way to more sophisticated designs—and the racing car of one day became the touring car of the next.

During the years from 1900 to 1914 innumerable automobile factories mushroomed all over the world. Inveterate optimists followed highly unconventional lines of thought, and compressed air, clockwork, liquid gas, and so on are mentioned as sources of power in the catalogues of those halcyon days. More than 700 makes were on the market, although many of these disappeared during the economic crisis of 1909.

During this period of vast expansion the motorcar began to attract the attention of the authorities. Neither the authorities nor the politicians showed any understanding of the automobile, let alone any sympathy. Nor did they show any great foresight. Their only interest was purely fiscal, and even that was halfhearted until, contrary to all their expectations, the automobile be-

The Gordon Bennett Cup

came so popular that later Ministers of Finance could profitably impose totally unwarranted taxes on car owners.

Even before this official animosity toward the motorcar found expression, the first motorcar club, the *Automobile Club de France,* was formed in 1895. Its original purpose was sporting and social, but the increased reliability and use of the automobile brought to the fore a number of traffic problems and matters affecting international travel. Since, too, the automobile was becoming a prime target for taxation, the character of the motoring clubs underwent a change, and they became organizations for furthering and protecting the interests of motorists; their principal task was to insure that the motorcar was accorded its rightful place in the community and in international circulation.

While motoring politics were still in embryo, the outlines of a proper automobile industry were beginning to take shape. In the early, chaotic attempts at producing the basic designs on an industrial scale, the larger and older firms held a leading position by reason of their greater technical experience. Some of them licensed subsidiaries abroad, and wideawake financiers tried to carve out empires stretching across national frontiers. *Adolphe Clément,* for example, controlled the French tire industry, had factories built to make his products under license in Britain and Italy, and was a founder member of the British firm of *Clément-Talbot Ltd.* In 1919 this firm amalgamated with the French *Darracq* company, whose automobiles were manufactured in the first decade of the twentieth century by *Opel* in Germany and *Alfa* in

Italy. The following year, the famous *Sunbeam* company of Wolverhampton joined the group, and the resultant S.T.D. combine was to be a major force in the European automotive industry until financial difficulties arose in 1935.

The golden age before 1914 also brought fresh blood into the young industry; the newcomers, free from preconceived ideas, sought to bring automobile engineering to full maturity. Three of them stand head and shoulders above the rest, and it would be hard to find three more completely different personalities than *Henry Ford, Henry Royce,* and *Ettore Bugatti.* They were alike only in their freedom from the ties of tradition; each went his own way and made his own decisive contribution to the shaping of the motorcar.

Henry Ford was an austere fanatic, combining such contradictory notions as far-reaching democracy and strict dictatorship. He embarked on the building of a "people's car" a full fifty years before this became an accepted idea, and carried his plans through at a time when the automobile was the preserve of a narrow circle of wealthy sportsmen. His immortal Model T came on the market in 1908 at a price of eight hundred and fifty dollars, and was produced for almost 19 years without any major changes in its unorthodox specification; it might well be called the greatest success the automobile industry has ever known. It was admired and despised, it was lauded to the skies and pilloried as a laughing stock; but no job was ever too hard for a Ford Model T, and no ill treatment was ever too much for its simple mechanical design. This automobile intro-

The idea of the Automobile Club de France was hatched over the dinner table in 1895 by Baron van Zuylen, Count de Dion, and the editor Paul Meyan

duced motor transport to the masses and earned itself a unique place in history. It also brought mass production to the industry.

Henry Royce followed another and completely different path. He began his career as an electrical engineer, and after the motorcar had caught his fancy he built his first automobile in 1903–1904. There was nothing revolutionary about its design, but the craftsmanship and detail work showed such care that the vehicle stood out among its contemporaries.

In December 1904 Royce signed a contract with *C. S. Rolls & Co.*, a London firm of importers and agents, for the manufacture of four types of chassis under the name of *Rolls-Royce,* and the first car carrying the classic angular radiator left the workshop in Manchester while the contract was still under discussion. In the following year the firm of Rolls-Royce Ltd. was registered and the factory was moved to Derby in 1908. Late in 1906 the firm brought out the model which made the

initials **RR** famous throughout the world—the celebrated "Silver Ghost." It was to be nineteen years before the Silver Ghost series was replaced by new models.

Alongside his work on motorcars Royce was deeply involved in experimental metallurgy, and he produced the famous Rolls-Royce alloys which are now in use in automobile factories throughout the world. The building of aero-engines has a very special place in the history of the firm. During the 1914–18 war the factory was suddenly switched to war production, but Royce scornfully rejected the design drawings which the government had bought from France. Instead he built his outstanding 12-cylinder *Eagle* power plant in 1915, following his inviolable rule of "testing every single part until it broke."

When Royce died in 1933 he was Sir Henry Royce, although he always signed his name simply "H. Royce, Mechanic"; indeed, he was able with his own hands to file a hexagonal hub cap so accurately that precision instruments

Bugatti, Type 13

small village of Molsheim, near Strasbourg, in 1910. His first production model was something unheard-of at that time: a small, light car with a four-cylinder motor featuring overhead valves and an overhead camshaft, and built like a fine watch. Many very much larger cars were hard put to it to keep up with this midget, which had a guaranteed top speed of 50 miles an hour. This "Type 13" and another, larger car with chain drive were built until war broke out in 1914. Bugatti buried his latest models in the ground beneath his workshop and fled with his family in two racing cars to Italy. From there he went to France and placed his services at the disposal of the wartime industry of the Allies. He built airplane engines in Paris, and in private an eight-cylinder car engine, the elegant design of which heralded the end of the clumsy adolescence of the motorcar that had lasted from 1906 to 1914.

could detect no difference between any of the six sides. The cars are still made to the inexorable standards of quality laid down by their founder.

The third member of this great triumvirate, *Ettore Bugatti,* was one of the most colorful figures in the history of motoring. He was born in 1881 in Milan, the son of an artist, Carlo Bugatti, an eminent master of painting, sculpture, metalwork, and architecture. Ettore's grandfather had squandered the family fortunes beyond all hope of recovery in vain attempts at solving the mystery of perpetual motion, and with this background it is understandable that the son's mechanical ambitions were bitterly opposed. They proved too strong, however, and he built his first mechanical vehicle, a twin-engined tricycle, in 1898. This was immediately followed by a small carriage with four motors, planned and built by Bugatti himself down to the smallest detail. Within three years Carlo Bugatti was signing a contract with the *De Dietrich* factory at Niederbronn, Alsace, on behalf of his son (who was still under age). After working for a few years for this and other firms, Ettore Bugatti went into business on his own in the

Bugatti both anticipated and pursued the technical refinements resulting from the Grand Prix races and the *voiturette* events sponsored by the journal *L'Auto* for the smaller types of car. His time of greatness was to come later, however, and a factor of more immediate significance was the design by a Swiss engineer named *Ernest Henry* of engines for Peugeot between 1912 and 1914 which incorporated the features of the modern sports and racing car engine—inclined valves driven from twin overhead camshafts and spark plugs placed immediately above the pistons.

Racing brought about other technical innovations of more direct use in everyday motoring. Four-wheel brakes were first used by the Italian firm of

Isotta-Fraschini on the Indianapolis racetrack in 1910, and then by *Delage, Peugeot, Fiat,* and *Piccard-Pictet* (a Swiss make which has since disappeared) in Europe in 1914. Contributions to this progress were also made in Britain by *Crossley* and by *Argyll* and *Arrol-Johnston,* both Scottish firms. In the same year Fiat introduced the unit-built engine clutch and gearbox. Independent front wheel suspension was revived by *Sizaire-Naudin* in 1907, only to be forgotten again for fifteen years, and in 1907–1908 the American *Lee Chadwick* used forced fuel feed to the cylinder by means of a supercharger; this even had three stages, a refinement of design which was only to be used in modified form by European manufacturers many years later.

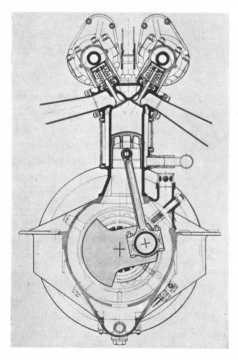

Cross section of Ernest Henry's Ballot engine

Just as the automobile was coming to maturity its peaceful development was interrupted. At the outbreak of war in 1914 the motorcar was still regarded rather skeptically by the general public, and the military experts looked on it with a mistrust bordering almost upon dislike. Although a few staff cars and heavy transport vehicles were in use, no real military role was allocated to, or even thought of, in connection with the automobile, the motorcycle, or–least of all—the flying machine.

The French master-stroke of improvisation during the battle of the Marne, when troop movements were carried out using Paris taxicabs, brought the motorcar to the notice of the army authorities and initiated a development that was to be of doubtful value for mankind. When the first tanks were sent into action on the Somme sector on September 15, 1916, the total mobilization of the automobile was complete.

Indirectly, however, the war had a more profitable influence upon technical progress. Automobile plants were converted for the production of ammunition, engines, aircraft, and other war material. Motorcars were used as ambulances and as transport and ordnance vehicles; automobile engineering was intimately bound up with the rapidly developing production of airplanes, and the store of engineering and production experience thus provided was an incalculable asset to the automobile industry when peace returned.

When the Armistice came in November 1918 automobile manufacturers had not only a solid background of technical knowledge which could be put to use for peacetime production, but also a generation of potential customers whom the war had familiarized with the everyday use of the internal combustion engine. While engineers were bringing a measure of technical logic to the arbitrary designs and chaotic production methods of the self-taught pioneers of the automobile, the world of high finance was moving into the factories with the investment needed for the mass production which alone would be capable of satisfying the limitless postwar demand for mechanical transport. The automotive industry, as opposed to the hand-built production of cars, spread to Europe from America.

The war had exploded the pattern of society, and in world production the luxury model was to occupy a very much less important place than the mass-produced automobile. Against this background a division emerged in the interwar years between cars from the conveyor belts of mass production and those from the workshops of smaller manufacturers. This division was not so marked at the beginning of the period, but it was thrown into clear relief by the economic depression of 1929 which knocked the legs from under the

The Somme, September 15, 1916

less solidly established concerns. Immediately after the war, however, there was a rosy glow of optimism everywhere. The large-scale industrial manufacture of automobiles began in the United States, where rationalized production methods were quickly adopted. In 1913, for instance, Ford produced more than 100,000 Model Ts, raised production to more than twice that number in 1914, and by 1919 was approaching the million mark. Other manufacturers also achieved production figures which demanded a very substantial investment of capital but at the same time gave a promise of dividends large enough to attract investors.

Even during the war the far-seeing kings of finance in the USA and Europe had sought to form vast cartels in the automobile industry. Some of these combines were built on shaky foundations, but others did possess a combination of technical and financial imagination which allowed them to survive competition in a merciless price war. The largest of these combines—*General Motors*—was founded by *William C. Durant*, who began his career as a maker of light horse-drawn carriages during the 1880s, acquired the bankrupt Buick factory in 1904 and completely reorganized it, made a fortune, and then began to explore the possibilities of controlling the whole of the automobile industry of the United States. Durant's basic scheme was to create a concern able to supply cars of any and every kind, considering that in this way he would be able to cover himself against variations in demand. First of all he tried to gather together Buick, Maxwell-Briscoe, Reo, and Ford, but was unable to find the necessary capital. Nevertheless on September 16, 1908 he registered the *General Motors Company* in New Jersey, and over a period of a couple of years managed to build up a most impressive bloc embracing Buick, Oldsmobile, Cadillac, and Oakland, apart from the now-forgotten names of Cartercar, Elmore, Marquette, Rainier, Rapid, Reliance, and Welch. General Motors moreover controlled various suppliers such as the Champion Ignition Company.

"Billy" Durant was an inveterate gambler in business, and in 1910 his hazardous financial maneuvers got G.M. into such dire straits that Buick's main creditor, the First National Bank of Boston, had to step in and Durant was obliged to slacken the reins. However, a quiet job on the board was the last thing that Durant had in mind for himself, and in 1910 he set up the *Little Motor Car Company* to build a low-price car designed by William H. Little. He followed this in 1911 with a car by *Louis Chevrolet*, and organized the *Chevrolet Motor Car Company*. Starting with these two concerns he built up a holding company which soon managed to control several other firms in the automobile industry. By 1915 Durant was able to group all his newly acquired interests under a new holding company called the *Chevrolet Motor Company*. His next move was to buy up G.M. shares with a view to gaining control of that concern when the bank relinquished control in 1915. He was successful, and 1916 saw Durant back in General Motors as president of the company, which strictly speaking belonged to the Chevrolet Motor Company. Two years later this financial subterfuge was regularized by

W. C. Durant (1860–1947)
Founder of General Motors

the creation of *General Motors Corporation*, which covered the whole of Durant's new empire.

Durant was seized with the general optimism of the postwar era and immediately launched upon a fresh round of risky transactions. He overreached himself so far that the brief crisis of 1920 brought him to the verge of bankruptcy. As things stood, Durant's personal ruin would have taken General Motors with it; but the *Du Pont Company* stepped in, and took over Durant's shares together with all his liabilities on condition that he resigned.

But still Durant did not disappear from the automobile industry. With admirable fighting spirit he tried to set up a third empire, this time under his own name, but his plans fell through. When the Depression of 1929 arrived *Durant Motors* was already a dying concern, and the crisis did no more than give the *coup de grâce*.

"Billy" Durant never recovered from this blow. His later role in the automobile industry was a modest one, and he

29

died in 1947, a forgotten figure from the turbulent youth of the industry; but he deserves to be remembered as a far-sighted and adventurous personality—perhaps too adventurous. General Motors was consolidated after the resignation of Durant, and quickly became the world's biggest manufacturer of automobiles. Assembly plants were set up in numerous countries in order to maintain exports in the face of increased trading restrictions, and G.M. also acquired *Vauxhall* in England in 1925 and *Opel* in Germany in 1929.

The basis of these vast concerns was a desire to conquer the market by being able to supply a wide choice of different automotive types. If sales dropped off in one sector of production, then hopes could be pinned on the remainder. Other manufacturers tried to reach the same goal by means of a single model which could be kept in production with constant reductions in price and gradual detail improvements. Both philosophies persist today, and are not limited to any one type of car; but the smaller, popular model has lent itself to both carefully calculated mass production and the more daring flights of the designers' imagination.

Since the automobile became a technical reality toward the end of the nineteenth century, the possibilities for creating a small, economical car for the man in the street had occupied the minds of many designers and businessmen. The earliest light cars were closely related to the motorcycle, and met with great popularity. Gradually, however, the small, single-cylinder car was felt to be too crude and primitive, as buyers even in the lower price range became more critical, and by 1914 the

original *voiturette* was beginning to disappear from the scene. The future trend toward small but well-designed cars was shown by the little Bugatti and the "Bebé" which Peugeot brought out in 1912 under Bugatti license.

Nevertheless, the boundless optimism of the first carefree days of peace put fresh life into a very light and utterly simple type of automobile known as the *cyclecar,* which had come on the scene in 1911 and allowed almost any engineering workshop to go into the car manufacturing business. With countless variations, the recipe for these cheerful little cars was as follows: a slender chassis, often made of wood, ultra-light and rickety bodywork, three or four spindly wheels, a motorcycle engine, chain or belt drive, or possibly some ingenious system using friction discs, wire and bobbin steering, and brakes which did anything but brake. Makes like the *Bédélia, Elfe, G.N., Cumbria, Tamplin, Imp, Woods Mobilette,* and many others were on the market before and after the war, and it is rather sad to record that they have all vanished. Only a few of their makers managed to survive the industrial developments of the twenties, and that only at the expense of the individuality which made their products so charming and so exasperating. Some of the makes of cyclecar were real curiosities, and had not the slightest chance of survival when proper cars such as the Morris, Citroën, and Austin could be supplied at competitive prices.

William Richard Morris, now *Lord Nuffield,* took only a few years to graduate from making bicycles and motorcycles to the manufacture of automobiles. His first model, the "Oxford," was presented to the public in the New Year of 1913 (with an engine block made of wood because the engine manufacturer was not quite ready!). A few months later the supply difficulties had been ironed out, and the first Morris with its characteristic rounded "bull-nose" radiator took the road. The same radiator was featured on the postwar models, production of which was soon so well organized that the price could be brought down to £330 ($1650) for a two-seater by 1923, and even lower—to £240 ($1200)—in 1926. The robust design of the car, and what the firm's catalogue for 1923 called its "impeccably good manners," won the make immense popularity and an almost legendary place in the history of British motoring.

The same character was to be found in the model which was brought out by *André Citroën* in 1919 and put into mass production the following year. Citroën was an industrialist, not one of the pioneers of the age of motoring, and he started out in car manufacture with the "Type A" designed by *Jules Salomon*. This was joined, in 1922, by the immortal "5 CV," better known as the "Citron" or "Clover-leaf." Citroën succeeded in carrying out what De Dion and Darracq had attempted, and introduced two revolutionary factors into European automobile production: mass production using special machine tools, and a small car which despite its size was reliable and sturdy to the point of indestructibility. Some of these original Citroën models are still to be seen on the roads of France: they steadily reel off kilometer after kilometer to mark up an astronomical total.

Aviette cyclecar

Both the Morris and the Citroën were, by today's reckoning, automobiles with medium-sized engines (1500 cc and 1400 cc respectively). But by the standards of the time of their appearance they had very small power units, and the engine of *Herbert Austin's* "Seven" must have seemed minute when it appeared at the London Motor Show in 1922 with only half the cubic capacity of the other two. Austin originally worked with Wolseley, but started up on his own in 1905. At first his production program varied a good deal, but the "Seven" met with such an overwhelming response that it remained in production until 1939. This was because it combined small size with low price and straightforward, durable machinery in a well-thought-out design suitable for large-scale production.

Lord Nuffield (W. R. Morris)

André Citroën (1878–1935)

These three automobiles were typical though by no means unique examples of the period from 1919 to 1930, which completed the transition from craft production to an industry proper. Until the economic crisis of 1929, cars were characterized by such abundant exuberance that they can well be termed "Vintage Cars."

If the better automobiles made during the 1920s occupy a respected niche in history, it is not just because they represented a lavish use of materials and labor and were of imposing architecture. The reason is to be found rather in the gradual but considerable accumulation of basic "know-how" by their designers and in an individuality of thought which industrial methods had not yet laid low. These cars embodied and continued the technical progress of an earlier age.

Seen in a wider context, it might well be acknowledged that no other single contribution to the mechanical specification of the automobile had more popular significance than *Charles F. Kettering's* electric "self-starter," which was first supplied as standard equipment by Cadillac in 1912. It made it possible for anyone to start up an automobile engine without risking painful, physical harm.

On the other hand, it was just as great a problem to bring the car, which had been started up so easily, to a standstill, and four-wheel brakes when they arrived were such a vast improvement over older systems that automobiles fitted with them were obliged in many countries to wear a red triangle on the back as a warning to others to exercise due care.

Little by little hydraulic brakes were also adopted, oil pipes gradually replacing the mechanical braking system with its less reliable cables and complicated layout of rods.

Kettering made a further important contribution to the popularization of the automobile in 1928 when he produced the synchromesh gearbox, which demanded a less delicate mechanical touch on the part of the driver. Designers on the fringe of the industry were already deep in speculation over the possibility of making gear-shifting completely automatic, although the majority continued to follow the general trend and build automobiles in a style which was in direct line with traditional ideas.

The chassis frame was the accepted basis for a motorcar, and hardly any designers dared to adopt a different solution, or even to make their chassis stiff enough for good road-holding. The hard springing in general use demanded that the whole automobile should be able to flex, and low-pressure tires went some way toward compensating for the uncomfortable nature of the springing.

Bugatti was one of the few who appreciated the merits of a really stiff frame, and as a result he was able to endow his products with vastly superior road-holding, although without making any concessions to such effeminate considerations as comfort. In most other cases the contact between the wheels and the road surface was insured by a balance between the vehicle's sprung and unsprung weight which was based on experience; success was often purely fortuitous. The engaging characteristics of the better cars of the 1920–30 period stemmed from a large, quiet-running engine and comfortable steering with a quick and precise action due to the main weight of the car being concentrated near the center. If the weight of an automobile is at one or other of the ends, it will be less ready to respond quickly to movements of the steering wheel, and when it does finally come, the response will tend to be rather too violent.

This period also brought the first serious attempts at building bodywork with aerodynamic properties, initially on a purely experimental and empirical basis and then on more solid, scientific principles. The welded-steel body began to oust the coach-built bodies in which sheets of metal were fixed on a wooden framework; these new bodies did much to overcome the twisting of the slender chassis frame, and introduced new methods of construction which used the bodywork as a partially or wholly self-supporting shell without any real chassis at all. *Lancia* blazed the trail in 1922 with their "Lambda"; it was a car in which the bodywork was reduced to a thin skin covering a stiff, integral construction which made independent front-wheel suspension at once desirable and advantageous.

In the short span of years which separated the end of one war from the outbreak of the next a great number of distinguished automobiles saw the light of day. True, quite a few of the great names of those days no longer exist, but they are still surrounded with an aura of respect which amounts almost to uncritical awe.

In the upper price ranges, for example, were *Cadillac, Cord, Cunningham, Duesenberg, Kissel, Lincoln, Packard*, and *Stutz* from the USA. In Europe the tone was set by France and Great Britain with makes like *Bugatti, Delage, Delahaye, Farman, Hispano-Suiza, Hotchkiss, Panhard & Levassor, Talbot-Darracq*, and *Voisin*, and *Daimler, Lanchester, Napier, Rolls-Royce*, and *Sunbeam* respectively. British sports cars such as the *Aston-Martin, Invicta, Lagonda, MG* (developed from the Morris), and *Vauxhall 30/98* were greatly favored; more than any other, however, it was the *Bentley* which was the epitome of a "vintage" car and was, at the same time, a type inevitably doomed to disappear during the economic depression of 1929–31. Rolls-Royce took the firm over, and when the name was revived it had become "The Silent Sports Car"—a mournful epitaph for a car whose deep, burbling exhaust note betrayed long experiment and development.

Belgium made her contribution to the illustrious cars of the twenties with the *Minerva, Métallurgique, Excelsior*, and other makes which have long since vanished. Holland had her *Spy-*

*Rumpler
"Teardrop," 1921*

ker, and among those from Italy were the *Ansaldo* and *Alfa Romeo*. This last started relatively uninterestingly, building under license from Darracq, but was brought to the fore by a railway engineer, *Nicola Romeo,* through outstanding results in motor racing. Apart from this, Italy also had the impressive *Isotto-Fraschini*.

Germany was hampered by the chaos of the postwar years. German industry was bowed under the crushing effects of revolution and inflation, and in the remains of what had been the Austro-Hungarian monarchy, too, economic conditions were not conducive to the pioneering work which *Dr. Hans Ledwinka* was doing with *Tatra*.

Another of the Central European geniuses of the motorcar, *Ferdinand*

Auto Union racing car, 1936

Porsche, worked with Daimler-Benz, when these two makes were merged in 1926. Two years previously the *Daimler-Motoren-Gesellschaft* and *Karl Benz & Cie., AG* had formed a joint company as a form of insurance against the unstable conditions prevailing in Germany. Daimler was dead, but Benz lived to see the fusion of the two concerns which, had it happened earlier, might well have made a considerable difference to the course of automobile history. No immediate technical results came from the union of the life-work of the two pioneers, and the new marque of Mercedes-Benz developed quietly for a number of years until political upheaval in Germany brought in its train a technical revolution, which to a very great extent emerged on the motor racing circuits.

During the early twenties *Ballot, Fiat,* and *Duesenberg* were the leading racing makes, and a number of important new features were subjected to thorough testing—hydraulic brakes, coil ignition, alcohol-gasoline mixtures, and superchargers. *Sunbeam, Alfa Romeo,* and *Delage* led the field in the succeeding years but their motors inspired more respect than their chassis.

In 1924 Bugatti showed his famous "Type 35" for the first time; this was an 8-cylinder 2-liter car which swept the board thanks to its superb chassis design. His subsequent "Type 51," which featured twin overhead camshafts, maintained the lead although hard pressed by the Alfa Romeos and the new Italian make of *Maserati*. However, when *Mercedes-Benz* and *Auto Union* made their re-entry and entry, respectively, into motor racing in 1934 with models which completely shattered the general conception of what was possible in the art of building competition cars, Bugatti and Maserati were reduced to the ranks of the "also-rans." Even the professional racing organization *Scuderia Ferrari,* which counted some of the most famous drivers of the day as members of its team—Tazio Nuvolari, Achille Varzi, Louis Chiron, Guy Moll, Carlo Felice Trossi, and many others—could make no impression on the German supremacy, in spite of full support from Alfa Romeo, for whom they acted as an official racing team.

Until that time motor racing had been more or less personal rivalry between a handful of manufacturers and some well-to-do private owners. When the Nazis came to power in Germany motor racing was made a part of their propaganda effort at home and abroad. Both leading German makers were given profitable armaments contracts so that they could spend their surplus on racing, and their engineers were able to make a radical breakaway from current ideas on springing and suspension, and to develop engines which seemed at the time better suited for installation in fighter planes than in automobiles. As soon as the inevitable teething troubles of the new cars were overcome, their revolutionary design was clearly seen to be justified; their "obliteration" of the vaunted Alfa Romeos and the inspired designs of Bugatti during the years 1936–39 proved the value of the new ideas.

The theory behind these drastic changes in chassis design had been known for several years, and a few factories had for some time been using independent suspension systems (with varying degrees of success) for the front wheels or for all four wheels. The problem of maintaining contact between the wheels and the ground, and the handling characteristics of the car, had been exhaustively and scientifically studied by a British-born US engineer, *Maurice Olley,* around 1930, but the theories which he had formulated had not yet been put to practical use. The majority of automobiles were still not built stiff enough to obtain the maximum benefit from a system of independent springing, and when General Motors introduced its so-called "knee-action" in 1933, the comfort of the ride at low speeds profited far more than did the car's fundamental handling characteristics. The economic upheavals of the Depression years did nothing to encourage technical progress in the automobile industry during the early thirties, and only a few really new features reached the production stage before the demand for armaments claimed the design capabilities of the engineers for other tasks.

One new idea was brought out in 1934 by Citroën, when their previous types were abandoned in favor of a front-wheel drive model "7A" which, in its own field, caused as much of a

Tazio Nuvolari's Maserati, 1933

sensation as did the German racing cars. Front-wheel drive, independent suspension by means of torsion bars, removable cylinder liners, and an integral, chassisless steel body combined to make up a specification of unprecedented boldness; but it succeeded so well that the factory was able to keep its "Traction-Avant" in production without any major changes for 23 years.

Maurice Olley

Bugatti's "Type 57," also introduced in 1934, was perhaps rather less epoch-making, for this independently minded designer always remained entirely unfettered by theoretical orthodoxy, and stubbornly built his cars according to his own ideas and as a kind of artistic, craftsman's exercise. Nevertheless his sporadic output often stole the limelight from the cars of other makers, and the Type 57 was a totally unexpected combination of the uncompromising characteristics of his earlier models coupled with real comfort and style. Bugatti had succeeded in concentrating all his experience and genius in a refined and elegant automobile which was able to satisfy the driver's every mood, and which followed unmistakably classic lines, while at the same time being so unorthodox in design that it still appears modern in many of its features.

Two years later a significant contribution to the motoring scene came from Italy when *Fiat* presented their diminutive "500," which had been created by *Dante Giacosa*. Although no direct connection can be traced between Ettore Bugatti and the Fiat "Topolino," it would not be too farfetched to draw a line from the Bugatti Type 13, through the Peugeot "Bébé" of 1912, the Citroën "5 CV," and the Austin "Seven" to the "Topolino."

This little car, which soon won enormous popularity, was one of those designs which created motoring history, opening up fresh perspectives by carrying two people and their luggage over quite long distances at an acceptable speed and with unbelievably modest fuel consumption.

Germany, too, provided a useful impetus to the solution of a problem which still remains topical—the design of a small car which is cheap to buy and cheap to run. The first German attempts in this direction had attained only a limited success, for they had been too unorthodox and the potential market was too small. When the German automobile industry found its legs again after 1930 the picture altered, and a Danish engineer, *Jørgen Skafte Rasmussen*, explored fresh avenues with the *D.K.W.* which had not only front-wheel drive but a two-cycle engine as well.

In 1932 D.K.W. joined with *Horch, Wanderer,* and *Audi* to form *Auto*

Union, and the group took over Dr. Ferdinand Porsche's plans for the rear-engined racing car which, together with the Mercedes-Benz, gave Germany her prewar prestige on the racing circuits and contributed to the upsurge of the automobile industry in Germany after 1935.

Dr. Porsche later left Auto Union in order to devote his time entirely to the development of a cheap family car. By 1938 his *Kraft durch Freude* car had passed the prototype stage, but it only went into mass production for civilian use, as the *Volkswagen,* after it had become painfully clear why Adolf Hitler had been so keen to re-establish the German automobile industry and to dominate motor sport.

The remaining European manufacturers and the powerful American industry brought out their various models during this period without reaching any really clear-cut results. The experience gained in motor racing did have a certain effect on the work of those designers who were more ready to accept progress. The shape of automobile bodies tended toward less drag, but firms who sought fundamentally new ways of doing things were few and far between.

Not long before America's entry into the Second World War General Motors launched automatic gear-changing in the form of "Hydramatic" transmission, which was based on the much earlier design work of *Herman Föttinger.* Similar ideas had long been in the minds of many engineers, and from 1931 onward the British Daimler was supplied with an oil clutch and a mechanical pre-selector gearbox which provided many of the advantages of a fully automatic transmission without leaving the choice of gear at any given moment to a mechanism which, in its blind infallibility, is incapable of thinking intelligently for itself. The results of the technical reorientation toward the end of the thirties had not however begun to show before war broke out.

Much of the experience gained by automobile engineers in the days of peace—and not least in sporting events —was now of decisive importance in adapting their designs for military purposes, and this experience was supplemented by new and dearly bought knowledge. Many problems which were unsolved or even barely formulated in 1939 were solved by the greater intensity of wartime research and the availability of men and materials regardless of cost. An example of this is the turbine engine, the fundamental principles of which had long been known although the practical realization had been hampered by insuperable difficulties of both a technical and financial nature. During the war turbine and jet engines were needed for military purposes in fighter aircraft, and their development was pushed ahead so that they were in use many years earlier than might otherwise have been the case.

The war also added an entirely new twig to the many-branched family tree of the motorcar when the *Jeep* was born. An easy-to-handle, uncomplicated, and extremely sturdy, light military vehicle was badly needed, and the experimental model designed by *American Bantam* and known as the "G.P. (General Purpose) Vehicle" was chosen from among those put forward by a

Willys 'Jeep', produced from 1941 onward

number of the big American manufacturers. It was put into production in a number of factories, notably *Willys-Overland,* so quickly that only a few months separated the drawing-board stage and the front line.

When the cease-fire came in 1945 the automobile factories had been either destroyed by bombing or converted to a purely wartime type of production. A tired, battered world was able to reorganize its broken industry only slowly in the face of the overwhelming difficulties caused by shortages of materials and a lack of skilled manpower. The first European postwar models followed, by and large, the 1939 specifications, and these came on the market in numbers which bore no relation to the vast demand that existed for them. The American industry had not been working under wartime conditions for quite as long, and its first peacetime

models had a quite overwhelming effect on a destitute Europe where they were unobtainable for lack of hard currency.

The end of the war brought a dull, gray reality instead of the bright plastic dream world that many had prophesied. New cars were one of the most glowing of these dreams, and the much-disparaged "dollar grin" treatment with chromium-plated frills over shiny, brightly-colored cellulose, was clearly a reaction to khaki and matt camouflage paint. But they brought no technical innovations.

In Europe the lead was taken by Italy. Disregarding material difficulties and political unrest, she brought about a renaissance of the automobile with sophisticated designs and elegant bodywork which attracted attention and admiration at the first European automobile show to be held after 1945. Scarlet-painted racing cars were brought out from their wartime hiding places and their supremacy gave the Italian industry further invaluable prestige. Alfa Romeo and Maserati were joined by a new make when *Enzo Ferrari,* who had been at the head of the Scuderia Ferrari of earlier years, began building cars at Modena: with a supreme disregard for the economic conditions which led most other manufacturers to think in terms of small, cheap models, Ferrari built costly and complicated cars which pointed to new horizons. Other Italian factories showed similar optimism, but some of them risked their luck too far and disappeared from the scene for a time or altogether, leaving behind them a shower of sparks from technical fireworks.

The French automotive industry, too,

passed through several troubled years, and the first automobile shows held in Paris were marked more by fantasy than by down-to-earth designs. However, the little rear-engined "4 CV" from the nationalized Renault works and the Panhard & Levassor "Dyna" showed a complete understanding of the current need for economical transport, and with the "2 CV"–dubbed the "citron pressé"—which was brought out in 1948 Citroën reduced the automobile to its acceptable minimum in a distinctive and cleverly designed vehicle. French cars in the upper price bracket, however, were passing through such lean times that the few models that did circulate around the various shows were rather like a squad of old soldiers being marched round and round to give the impression of numbers; finally they faded out altogether.

In Germany the automobile industry was completely disorganized, and its first serious comeback was made in 1950 with prewar models, including the Volkswagen, which won a quite unprecedented popularity. The industry both contributed to and profited from the West German *"Wirtschaftswunder,"* and as the "economic marvel" progressed, so did the needs and demands of the German public for automobiles. The "minimum motoring cars" met the same fate as the corresponding models of the 1920s, and were replaced by cars which satisfied more stringent demands for performance and comfort and at the same time incorporated the growing store of practical and theoretical experience.

The industry in Great Britain was hampered by restrictions and by its own ingrained traditionalism. Genuine

Healey, 1946

postwar designs were a long time in coming from the big manufacturers, but gradually the industry changed course to follow up on its initial success in the export markets.

The years since the war have seen a vast expansion in the international automobile industry, and increased competition has brought about a good deal of merging and reshuffling. Some makes have vanished from the scene, some new ones have appeared, and others again have joined forces in technical and economic cooperation—sometimes within and sometimes across national frontiers.

Automobiles are entering more and more into the fabric of present-day living, and only seventy years after the birth of the industry there are more than one hundred million cars in use all over the world. The automobile industry occupies a key position in international economics, and since 1945 technical progress has been so rapid that only a very few of the cars made

VW with Ghia body—a workaday car in its Sunday best

Modern disc brakes were developed through racing

before the war can stand comparison with their modern counterparts. Recent trends have been toward even better braking (including the advent of disc brakes and a more suitable distribution of the braking effect between the front and rear wheels), simplified automatic transmissions, more precise steering and suspension, and new types of motors such as the free-piston engine and, potentially, the turbine engine.

Although basic principles still remain unaltered, all the main features bear witness to developments which have made it possible for manufacturers today to mass-produce cars which have a standard of performance, economy, handling, safety, and comfort superior to that of many earlier masterpieces of car design.

Safer handling properties and simplification of the controls may, however, bring the human element out of phase with developments. The cars themselves have become easier to manage, but the increasing density of traffic calls for a keener realization of human and mechanical capabilities and limitations. The glorious freedom of the automobile, in a day and age which is rapidly becoming regimented and regulated in all its aspects, must not be thrown away through neglect of the responsibility which progress will do little to lessen. This would be a sorry betrayal of the efforts of the pioneers, and lead to a state of affairs which would measure up neither to dreams of the past, the realities of the present, nor the hopes for the future.

The dual monarchy of Austria-Hungary (which also included Czechoslovakia) was the homeland of a farsighted designer of a gasoline automobile, *Siegfried Markus* (1831-98). His first car is said to have covered a distance of 200 yards in 1870/71, and was succeeded by an improved version some four years later. Recent research casts some doubt on the exact date of the Markus cars, and the final model should, perhaps, be dated around 1890. Markus was highly gifted technically, but not sufficiently down-to-earth to produce a practical and usable car; his automobiles were in fact preliminary studies for airship engines.

There is no discernible direct link between Markus's experiments and the quite substantial automotive industry which grew up in Austria and Czechoslovakia before the outbreak of war in 1914. Both independent factories and branches of foreign firms were well established when the lights of Europe went out, but after 1918 only a few firms were able to survive in the shattered remains of the Hapsburg empire. The most viable of them merged during the years between 1918 and 1939, and the rest disappeared.

Engineers from Austria-Hungary—*Ferdinand Porsche, Hans Ledwinka*, and *Edmund Rumpler*—had a very considerable influence on automotive design in Central Europe in the period after 1920, their pioneering work covering motors, chassis, and bodywork. Porsche's main achievements are described on p. 44, Ledwinka's on pp. 43, 54, and 55. Rumpler is known in particular for his aircraft designs and a most unorthodox car, shown on p. 34.

The *Markus* car (1875 ?), one of the oldest gasoline-powered cars. The 1-cyl. watercooled 4-cycle engine (100×200 mm, 1570 cc; 4″×7⅞″, 95.9 cu. in.) gave ¾ hp at 500 rpm, and can still move the ¾-ton car at about 2½ mph. Its electric ignition, carburetor, and mechanical valve opening foreshadowed many later cars. It now stands, in running order, in Vienna Technical Museum.

Austro-Daimler 20/30 HP, 1918,
4-cyl. 90×140 mm, 3560 cc; 3⅝″×
5½″, 217 cu.in.

The first models to come from
the *Oesterreichisches Daimler Motoren
Gesellschaft* were German Daimlers
(Mercedes) built under license.
After Ferdinand Porsche took
over the technical direction of the
firm in 1906 they built their own
highly interesting designs, until
the make merged with Steyr and
Puch during the 1930s.

Puch "Voiturette," 1910

Johann Puch established a bicycle factory in Graz in 1899, and soon after
started building motorcycles which
won innumerable races and paved the
way for production of cars and
trucks. The death of the founder in
July 1914, and the economic chaos
which followed 1918, led to amal-
gamation first with Austro-Daimler
and later with Steyr. Puch still produce motorcycles within this combine.

Puch "Model VIII," which won the make fame in
Austrian Alpine Trials between 1907-14.

Steyr, 1922
embodied the orthodox, sturdy design of this make.

Joseph Werndl founded an armaments factory in Styria in 1853. In 1920 cars were included in the factory's products, and the Czech designer *Hans Ledwinka* provided a specification which combined sound, orthodox principles with forward-looking ideas. Ledwinka went back to Czechoslovakia two years later to take charge of the distinctive range of *Tatra* cars; in 1951, after many years spent in prison there, he returned to Austria as Technical Director of Steyr-Daimler-Puch.

The **Steyr "30"** was the classic Viennese taxi. *Ferdinand Porsche* joined Steyr in 1929 and modified this model before turning to the design of more modern types (see p. 44).

Gräf & Stift, 1925
This long-established horse-carriage firm joined the automotive industry in 1895, and after the war built, among others, an 8-cylinder model. Later the Model MF6 was made under a Citroën license; production of passenger cars ceased around 1935.

Denzel "WD Seriensuper 1300," 1959, a much-modified version of the VW made since 1948 by Wolfgang Densel of Vienna.

Steyr-Puch "500," 1960 (*left*) and the larger models in the current Steyr range use Fiat bodies with the firm's own engines. The S-D-P concern is the successor of *Austro-Fiat,* but the "500" engine (2-cyl. 66×70 mm, 479 cc; $2\frac{5}{8}'' \times 2\frac{3}{4}''$, 26.7 cu. in.) is Ledwinka's work.

Austria

Ferdinand Porsche (1875-1951) began his career in 1898 with *Jacob Lohner* of Vienna, building gasoline-powered cars with electric motor transmission. In 1906 he moved to *Austro-Daimler,* where he produced the famous "Prince Henry" sports car (4-cyl. ohc 105 × 165 mm, 5714 cc; 4⅛″ × 6¼″, 348.4 cu.in.). Porsche went to Daimler in 1923 and designed many outstanding *Mercedes* and (later) *Mercedes-Benz* models. He left Daimler-Benz in 1929 and worked with *Steyr* until he set up on his own as a consultant and development engineer. This led to the *Auto Union* racing cars and the *Kraft-durch-Freude* car—alias the *VW*. In 1944 *Porsche Konstructionen GmbH* moved from Stuttgart to Gmünd in Austria, where the *Porsche* "356" was developed from the VW and ran in prototype form in 1948—the first car to carry his own name.

Lohner-Porsche, 1900, racing version, which won the Semmering hill-climb with the designer at the wheel. A powerful gasoline engine drove a dynamo supplying current to an electric motor in each wheel hub.

Sascha, 1922, was Porsche's light-car design for Austro-Daimler (4-cyl. 68.3 × 75 mm, 1099 cc; 2⅝″ × 3″, 67 cu.in.). Named after Count Sascha Kolowrat, who entered the car in the Targa Florio race in Sicily where Alfred Neubauer was well placed with the racing version of the marque.

Steyr "55," 1936, a water-cooled "back-to-front" VW designed by Porsche. A 4-cyl. 1000 cc (60 cu.in.) horizontally opposed motor at the front drove the back wheels which, as in Ledwinka's Tatra, were on swing axles.

Porsche "356," No. 1, 1948

Australia

Although cars were manufactured in Australia before 1900, it was not possible to build up any major production in the face of competition from more industrialized countries. The needs of the market were met from Europe and the USA.

In 1948 General Motors at Woodville started production of the Holden, a purely Australian make.

The **Pioneer** was built in Melbourne in 1897 by the "Australian Horseless Carriage Syndicate," the design following early European lines. Individual local features, however, can be seen in the kerosene motor and the swiveling front axle which allowed the car to turn on a dime. The high wheels recall early cars in the USA, where there was also a demand for automobiles with wheels which could cut through to the bottom of the morasses which passed for roads.

Pioneer, 1898

Holden's first model in 1948/49 was fitted with a 6-cyl. motor (76 × 79.4 mm, 2170 cc; $3'' \times 3\frac{1}{8}''$, 132.5 cu.in.), and had a sturdy, chassisless body with stout suspension. Production reached 20,000 the first year. The basic specification has remained the same, although the body has been modernized.

Holden, 1960

The **Holden** of 1949 was, in appearance and mechanical design, a blend of European, American, and Australian ideas. The 1960 model (*left*) shows the changed lines which follow world fashion; annual production is 100,000.

45

A whole range of fine cars have reached the roads of the world from Belgium. Raw materials, technical experience, and capital were all at hand for the establishment of an automobile industry, which flourished from its beginnings before 1900 until 1914 and again between 1920 and the Depression. As developments made hand-production methods increasingly less profitable, the numerous Belgian factories had either to join forces or close down in the face of mass production from neighboring countries and the USA.

Many illustrious makes disappeared altogether, while others led a languishing existence as assembled products of foreign origin, although still keeping the old names. One or two firms made a brief reappearance after 1945, though their designs were not Belgian, and attempts to re-establish the automobile industry met with failure.

More than 60 different makes originated in Belgian factories, and names like *Pipe, Nagant, Excelsior, Belgica, Soméa,* and *SAVA* were well known and highly respected in their day. Others attained only parochial fame, while others again inspired more wonderment than confidence, for example the *Demati,* which was brought out in 1937 with front-wheel drive and rear-wheel steering.

Today they have all taken their place on the shelves of motoring history, reminders of initiative, mechanical imagination—and broken hopes.

Germain, 1908 (4-cyl. 102 × 110 mm, 3598 cc; 4″ × 4⅜″, 219 cu.in.). The firm built under *Daimler* and *Panhard* licenses from 1897. After 1903 they made their own cars, some with an electric gearshift.

Sylvain de Jong set up a factory in 1897 producing bicycles under the name *Minerva*. Two years later *S. de Jong & Cie* took up the manufacture of small engines and motorcycles, and in 1903 the firm's name was altered to *Minerva Motors Ltd.* At the same time plans were laid for series-production of a light car, and the first "Minervette" came on the market in 1905. Three years later manufacturing rights to the Knight double-sleeve motor were acquired and very fine automobiles were built using this power unit.

After De Jong's death in 1928, during the economic crisis Minerva weakened: in 1934 the make was merged with the *Impéria* concern to form the *Société Nouvelle des Automobiles Minerva,* but independence was lost and today Impéria-Minerva is only an assembly plant.

Minerva "5 HP," 1904
This single-cylinder model preceded the first "Minervette" series, and was soon joined by bigger types which competed in important races. The "Kaiserpreis" model of 1907 won the Circuit des Ardennes, but did less well in the earlier race for the Kaiser's Cup.

Minerva "Kaiserpreis," 1907, with speedster body (4-cyl. 145 × 120 mm, 8000 cc; 5⅞" × 4⅞", 487.8 cu.in.) made the make famous. It was replaced in 1908 by models with sleeve-valve motors.

Minerva "18 HP," 1913 (4 cyl. 90 × 130 mm, 3305 cc; 3⅝" × 5⅛"; 201.5 cu.in.; sleeve-valves), one of the early models which made the marque world-famous. Sleeve-valve Minervas kept in production into the 1930s, and were relatively quiet-running provided the motor was properly adjusted and not too badly worn; there was a characteristic cloud of smoke when a Minerva accelerated. The cars were noted for their sturdy build and smart trim, had a fine technical reputation, and were highly prized as status symbols.

"24 CV," 1925
6-cyl. 80×112 mm
3380 cc
(3⅛"×4⅜", 138 cu.in.)

During the twenties Minerva made three models: a 4-cyl. (80×112 mm, 2260 cc; 3⅛"×4⅜", 138 cu.in.) and two 6-cyl. models (80×112 mm, 3380 cc; 3⅛"×4⅜", 207 cu.in. or 90×112 mm, 4280 cc; 3⅝"×4⅜", 259 cu.in.). The two larger models were well-suited to dignified bodywork like the "Coupé de Ville" shown here. During the Depression the largest model was abandoned, and in 1930 a "22 CV" model was brought out with a 4-liter 8-cyl. sleeve-valve engine and some American components in the design.

The **"28 HP"** was introduced in 1930 with a 1500 mile Ostend-Marseilles-Ostend "Marathon" completed in 32 hours, 35 minutes. In this special short-chassis model the engine-power was raised from its normal 80 bhp at 3000 rpm to 130 bhp at 4000 rpm. With four passengers and luggage the car had a top speed of around 87 mph, and powerful mechanical servo-brakes permitted full use of this performance.

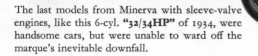

The last models from Minerva with sleeve-valve engines, like this 6-cyl. **"32/34HP"** of 1934, were handsome cars, but were unable to ward off the marque's inevitable downfall.

The last
Minervas:
"14HP" 4-cyl.
"21HP" 6-cyl.
"28HP" 8-cyl.
"32/34HP" 6-cyl.
"40HP" 8-cyl.

Vivinus "6HP," 1900 (2-cyl. 95×100 mm, 1420 cc; 3¾"×4", 86 cu.in.). This make was established in 1899, and lasted until World War I. Alexis Vivinus then went to work for Minerva. These automobiles were built under license in England as the *New Orleans,* and in France by *Georges Richard.*

Miesse, 1906 (3-cyl. steam engine). *Jules Miesse* sold his first steam-car in 1896, and thus became the first Belgian car manufacturer. Gasoline-powered vehicles were also built from 1900 onwards. The steam car was built in England 1902-13 as the *Turner-Miesse.* No passenger cars were made after 1926.

FN stands for Fabrique Nationale d'Armes de Guerre. Both cars and motorcycles have come from this large armaments firm at Herstal, Liège.

Excelsior merged in 1928 with Impéria, which had already swallowed up *Métallurgique* and *Nagant.* In 1934 the Impéria concern joined Minerva.

FN sports car, 1925/26, a worthy though not typical example of the small cars made 1900-35 by the Fabrique Nationale. Designs for the early models were by *P. de Cosmo,* who had worked for *Delahaye* and later made cars under his own name. A big, 8-cyl. FN in 1931 hastened the end of the make.

Excelsior, 1923 (6-cyl. 85×140 mm, 4770 cc; 3¼"×5½", 285 cu.in.)

Impéria-Abadal
1922 (4-cyl.
80 × 150 mm,
3000 cc;
3⅛″ × 6″, 182.9 cu. in.)

Métallurgique occupies a leading place among Belgium's proudest marques. The firm originally made railway equipment, but started building automobiles just before the turn of the century, delivering its first 2-cyl. cars in 1900. Later models were a good deal larger, and a "Métal" was a handsome and much-respected vehicle. Production ceased in 1927.

Impéria was set up a few years before the start of World War I, and was known after 1920 as *Impéria-Abadal*. In the 1920s the firm made large 4- and 8-cyl. cars, but the most interesting models were two smaller racing cars with 1100 and 1650 cc slide-valve engines. Neither these nor other technical star performers could ride out the Depression, however, and the standard models of the twenties were too uninspired to survive; an interesting, well-built motor had to pull an overheavy chassis, limiting performance. The manufacture of these automobiles under license in Britain was discussed but never consummated, and the financial transactions which brought together Métallurgique, Nagant, and *Arthur de Coninck's* illustrious make, Excelsior, under the Impéria name, also failed to revive the marque.

The fusion with Minerva in 1934 sealed the fate of both makes, although after 1935 a front-wheel drive *Adler* was built under license and called the Impéria. The name appeared again in 1948 with a front-wheel drive *Hotchkiss-Grégoire* design, and this system of drive was again the theme for the swansong of the Minerva in 1953. This time it was an Italian design, the *Cemsa-Caproni,* which for a few years was shown in vain at all the auto shows, was hailed as a sensation, was forgotten, and then revived in 1960 in slightly modified form as the *Lancia* "Flavia" (see pp. 155 and 161).

Métallurgique "12/40," 1925 (4-cyl.)

Métallurgique "40HP," 1912

Impéria "TA 8," 1948

Brazil is one of the main competitive markets for vehicles from Europe and the USA, and both are represented by local assembly plants making models which often differ in some respects from the domestic product. Yearly production runs at about 100,000 units, mostly trucks and agricultural and industrial vehicles. Some cars, such as the *Aero Willys,* are produced using designs which are about ten years old.

Aero Willys, 1961, built by the Brazilian subsidiary of Willys-Overland on the basis of the main factory's 1952 model (6-cyl. 79.4×88.9 mm, 2199 cc; $3\frac{1}{8}'' \times 3\frac{1}{2}''$, 161 cu.in.). The factory also builds the famous Jeep.

Canada has a substantial automobile industry centered in Toronto, where there are subsidiaries of the large US manufacturers. An early attempt to produce a purely Canadian industry was unsuccessful—Detroit was too close at hand—and slightly altered models are assembled and sold under Canadian names.

Russel-Knight, 1914
This 4-cyl. car with a sleeve-valve engine was one of the last made by the Canada Cycle & Motor Co., Toronto.

Ford "Meteor," 1955

51

Switzerland

Martini produced automobiles in series from 1899-1931, and from the beginning incorporated individual design features such as magneto ignition, constant-mesh gears, etc.

Switzerland—the letters on the nationality plate stand for "Confédération Helvétique"—managed to build up an automobile industry before 1914, with products which were of high quality although little known outside their own country. About twenty firms were established, the more vigorous lasting until the twenties and one remaining in business until 1934. The truck-building firms, however, survived the crisis years and have proved quite competitive. Apart from their high quality, Swiss makes showed a good deal of mechanical ingenuity in many details.

Martini, 1897, 2-cyl. experimental mode

Martini, 1899, with front engine

Saurer, 1898 (still making trucks)

Martini "Martinili," 1914, 4-cyl.

Ajax, 1906

Berna, 1912 (still making trucks)

Turicum "Roller," 1904, was steered with the feet, and otherwise controlled by means of levers for the friction gear and brake.

Martin Fischer (1866-1947) designed his first motor vehicle in 1904; it was a single-seater "Roller" ("scooter") which anticipated the mini-cars of today. His design approach was quite unorthodox, and in later *Turicum* cars he was constantly searching for fresh solutions. The motor (*above*) and chassis (*below*) of the 1910 model show the clear layout and characteristic friction transmission. A large wheel fixed to the motor output shaft drove a friction wheel which could be moved along a transverse shaft to give infinitely variable gearing from 4:1 to 1.07:1.

Turicum "12/15 HP," 1911, 4-cyl. 75 × 110 mm, 1940 cc; 3″ × 4⅜″, 118 cu.in.; 16 hp at 1800 rpm; friction transmission, top speed of about 22 mph. The firm was liquidated in 1913. Turicum is the Latin name for Zurich.

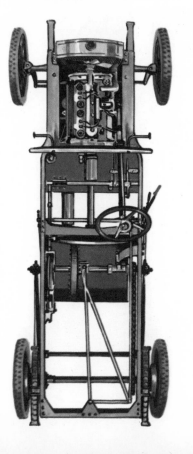

Pic-Pic, 1923, got its name from its manufacturers, *Piccard, Pictet & Cie,* which took up car production in 1906 in collaboration with *S.A.G.* (Société d'Automobiles à Genève). Production ceased in 1924.

Enzmann "506," 1958, a Swiss make of recent times, first seen at the Frankfurt Salon in September 1957. It features a doorless fiberglass body on a slightly modified VW chassis with a mildly tuned VW engine.

Czechoslovakia

Skoda "1100," 1947

Czech car design is notable for its lively imagination, disregard for convention, and deep reverence for *Hans Ledwinka*.

Laurin & Klement, 1905

Skoda "Octavia," 1961
4-cyl. 1089 cc (68×75 mm; $2\frac{3}{4}'' \times 3''$)
Backbone chassis, etc.

Aero, 1934, front-wheel drive, 2-cyl. 2-cycle 1000 cc (60 cu.in.)

Heavy industry in the Czech part of the dual monarchy of Austria-Hungary provided an ideal foundation for motorcar manufacture, and practical automobiles were being made before 1900 by the *Nesselsdorfer Waggonbau Fabrikgesellschaft* and *Laurin & Klement* (which became, respectively, *Tatra* and *Skoda*). Both makes introduced outstanding chassis and engine designs 1920-39. Several firms, including *Aero*, built 2-cycle motors. Hans Ledwinka's influence is evident in most makes—backbone chassis and independent suspension with swing axles at the rear. Makes such as the *Z*, *Walter*, *Praga*, *Jawa*, etc. have disappeared from the passenger-car market.

Aero-Minor, 1947
backbone
chassis,
2-cycle 2-cyl.
616 cc
(38 cu.in.)

Jawa, 1938
(Janecek-Wanderer)

Nesselsdorf, 1897

Tatra, 1931

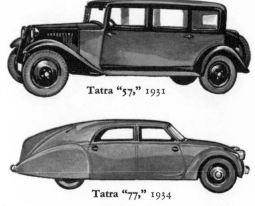

Tatra "57," 1931

Tatra "77," 1934

In 1921 Ledwinka returned from Steyr, and his Tatra "12" of 1923 featured a 2-cyl. air-cooled motor at the front, a backbone chassis, and i.r.s. with swing axles. In the 1933 "77" the 8-cyl. motor was put at the rear and in 1934 aerodynamic body-work was added. Early Ledwinka designs included hemispherical combustion chambers, four-wheel brakes, and rack-and-pinion steering.

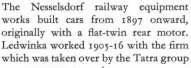

The Nesselsdorf railway equipment works built cars from 1897 onward, originally with a flat-twin rear motor. Ledwinka worked 1905-16 with the firm which was taken over by the Tatra group in 1921.

"Tatraplan," 1951, with a 4-cyl. 85×86 mm 1952 cc; $3\frac{1}{4}'' \times 3\frac{1}{4}''$, 120 cu.in. air-cooled engine was the first postwar model.

T-"603," 1961, V-8 2455 cc (151 cu.in.)

Germany's path to a central position in the automobile world has been anything but smooth. The pioneering work af *Carl Benz* and *Gottlieb Daimler* during the 1880s had very limited results in their own country, while France built up her own industry far more rapidly, using Daimler engines. At about the turn of the century German makes began to score technical and sporting triumphs, and by 1914 a well-established industry could be adapted to military purposes. The inflationary period after 1918 killed some of the older firms, and produced a few ephemeral makes and some with a longer life-span. Technical features between 1920 and 1939 ranged from rigid tradition to imaginative vision, and Germany gradually regained a leading position in the technical, sporting, trade, and military fields. When defeat came in 1945 the automobile industry was quite literally in ruins. However, car production both helped and profited from the astounding economic recovery of West Germany, although the number of producers has fallen to nine, and overoptimistic expansion, coupled with keener competition at home and abroad, have had their consequences. The annual production of cars in the Federal Republic today approaches 2,000,000.

Auto Union was formed during the crisis of the 1930s from three older makes: *Audi, Wanderer, Horch,* and the newer *DKW.*

Audi, 1920

DKW, 1928

Horch, 1927

Wanderer, 1910

R 1359

Nazi leaders' parade car
Horch "853," 1938/9, 8-cyl.

Audi, 1939

DKW, 1931

Wanderer, 1939

DKW, 1939

DKW, 1952

The Danish engineer *Jørgen Skafte Rasmussen* was the originator of the DKW. The letters stood for Damp-Kraft-Wagen, since Rasmussen's first design in 1916 was a light steam car. The two-cycle gasoline engine came originally from the DKW works in 1919 as a toy model engine, but *"Das Kleine Wunder"* grew into a motorcycle engine and was used in the first rear-wheel drive DKW car in 1928. Three years later the firm adopted front-wheel drive, which it has used ever since—still with a two-cycle engine, which has undergone substantial development.

Auto Union "1000"

DKW "Junior"

BMW "Dixi," 1928

BMW chassis, 1932

"303," 1200 cc (73 cu. in.) 1933

"315," 1500 cc (91.4 cu. in.) 1935

"327," 1971 cc (120.2 cu. in.) 1937

"328," 1971 cc (120.2 cu. in.) 1938

Around 1900 the *Fahrzeugfabrik Eisenach AG* made a car called the *Wartburg*. The firm was taken over soon afterward by BMW (Bayerische Motoren Werke), which in 1928 also absorbed the *Dixi* works which made the *Austin* "Seven" under license. This started BMW off on automobile production, and in 1932 they produced a design of their own with a 4-cyl. 800 cc (49 cu.in.) engine and independent suspension. A range of larger types were developed from this model, with handling characteristics and appearance which won the marque international fame, and the 6-cyl. 2-liter type 55 sports car of 1935 formed the basis for license production in England by *Frazer-Nash*. Soon after this the 4-cyl. models were abandoned, and from 1936-39 BMW made the "326," "327," and "328," the last two having a more sporting type of motor with hemispherical combustion chambers and inclined valves. The "328" was an outstanding sports car, with impressive performance and an unusual degree of comfort. A 3½-liter model, the "355," was just coming into production in 1939 but very few were made. After 1945 the factory moved from Eisenach to Munich.

B.M.W., "328" with streamlined racing bodywork based on Professor W. Kamm's experiments.

"700," 1959

"507," V-8 3168 cc, 82×75 mm; 194 cu.in., 3⅛"
×3"; 140 bhp at 4800 rpm (165 bhp in special
form). Max. speed 137 mph.

The first postwar model, the "501,"
was shown at Frankfurt in 1952 with
an improved "326" motor and a well-
designed but rather heavy chassis.
The styling was modern, although
somewhat bulbous, and production
was small. In 1954 came the "502,"
with an extremely up-to-date 2.6-liter
(157 cu.in.) V-8 engine.

From 1955 onward the BMW range included
sports cars, fitted with V-8 engines (2.6/3.2 liters;
157/195 cu.in.), while the more sedate "503" was
also supplied as an elegant convertible. Despite
excellent handling and beautiful workmanship the
large cars were difficult to sell, and for this reason
the factory concentrated from 1956 onward on a
development of the Italian *Isetta* "bubble-car"; the
BMW "600," which appeared in 1957, was an
independent contribution to the solution of the
special design problems of the mini-car. It was too

unconventional to be popular, but the "700" which
followed in 1959 looked so much like a conventional car that its unorthodox technical features
did not scare off the customers. The model underwent further development and became available
as a sports car. An entirely new 1½-liter (91 cu.in.)
4-cyl. model (82×71 mm; 3⅛"×2¾") was un-
veiled at the Frankfurt Salon in 1961, showing
clearly that this old-established factory has not
lost its technical inventiveness in spite of financially troubled years.

"503," 1955

BMW Isetta, 1956

"501," 1933

BMW "600," 1959

59

Germany

Hansa, 1905

Lloyd Elektro, 1910

Carl Friedrich-Wilhelm Borgward made his debut in the German car industry in 1917 via the *Bremer Reifenindustri*, which in 1924 began building three-wheeled two-cycle delivery "Blitzkarren." Two years later these developed into the first *Goliath* passenger car, and a new firm *Goliath-Werke Borgward & Co.* was established. In 1929 Carl Borgward acquired control of the failing *Hansa-Lloyd* company; this had been formed in 1914 from a merger of the *Hansa Automobilgesellschaft* (established in 1905) and the *Norddeutsche Automobil und Motoren AG (NAMAG)*, which prior to 1914 had a very wide range of *Lloyd* gasoline and electric cars for all purposes. The whole group was merged in 1938 under the title *Carl F.-W. Borgward Automobilwerke*, the Hansa name being used for passenger cars while Lloyd and Goliath were used initially for trucks.

Hansa-Lloyd "Trumpf AS," 1927

Goliath "Pioneer," 1926, with 1-cyl. 200 cc (12 cu. in.) ILO 2-cycle engine, 3-speed transmission.

Aerodynamic Hansa "1½ liter," 1937

Hansa "500," 1934, 2-cyl. 500 cc (30 cu. in.) air-cooled rear engine, four gears, swing axles.

Hansa "1100,"
1939

Hansa "1500," 1949

Lloyd
"LP 400," 1954

Goliath, 1950

Borgward started production again in 1948, and their first new model, the Hansa "1500," was shown at Geneva in 1949. The following year the first Goliath appeared, with a twin-cylinder 688 cc (42 cu.in.) two-cycle engine and front-wheel drive. This was joined in 1951 by the Lloyd "LP 300" (2-cyl. 386 cc [23 cu.in.] 2-cycle, front-wheel drive); the very spartan fabric bodywork earned it the nickname "Hansaplastwagen" (i.e. band-aid car). The model was aimed at satisfying elementary transport needs with strict economy, and as economic conditions improved it grew in size and improved in equipment until it finally lost its old identity. The larger models were renamed *Borgward*, and the Hansa name came and went. But despite a number of interesting contributions to car design, it gradually became clear that the firm's models were not catching on. The competition from other German makes was too fierce, and export markets found it hard to accept the distinctive, Germanic styling of the bodywork.

In 1961 Carl Borgward's dream faded, and his autocratic empire had to go into liquidation.

Borgward "Isabella," 1960

Goliath "1100," 1957

Lloyd "Arabella," 1961

Seen against the backdrop of technical history, *Gottlieb Daimler* appears as a very farsighted designer of engines. His contribution to the development of the automobile was the light, reliable, medium-speed gasoline engine. His designs formed the basis for the modern, high-revving engine, although Daimler was not aiming at producing an automobile engine—far less an automobile. He strove to create an all-purpose motor.

Carl Benz, on the other hand, was obsessed with the idea of a vehicle fitted with a gasoline motor, and worked single-mindedly on a design combining the individual components in a planned, organic whole. His basic patent, DRP 37,435, taken out on January 29, 1886, was for a "carriage with gas engine," whereas Daimler's main patent, DRP 28,022 of December 16, 1883, was for a "gas engine." The first Benz carriage represented a vital step in the development of the motorcar, and the designer cannot be blamed for the fact that a 3-wheeled vehicle is not classified as an automobile In 1885 no one knew what an automobile was. Daimler's first carriage was an improvisation for testing his all-purpose engine for boats, trains, airplanes, and so on. The breakthrough of the Daimler car was due to the "8 HP" model of his son *Paul Daimler,* which inspired *Wilhelm Maybach* to produce the first "*Mercédès*" of 1900-1901—the model which brought Daimler fame. Benz kept his original design for too long, and allowed it to be succeeded by somewhat undistinguished cars. Shortly before the union of the two marques the Daimler company was becoming set in its ways, whereas Benz showed a less traditional outlook, and when *Dr. Porsche* took over the technical control of Daimler-Benz, progress was made, progress that was to be followed by extremely rapid development through Mercedes-Benz' participation in Grand Prix racing from 1934 onwards.

Daimler experimental model, 1886

Benz "Patent carriage," 1886

Daimler "Stahlradwagen," 1889

"From here a star will rise," Daimler explained when the three-pointed star was painted as a device on the front of his house.

MERCÉDÈS JELLINEK

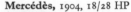

Cannstatt-Daimler "24 HP," 1899

Between the 24 HP model of 1899 (4-cyl. 106 × 156 mm; 4⅛″ × 6⅛″) and the "Mercédès" which was ready for test runs in November 1900 lies the borderline between the old and the new. The 24 HP was a monster of a car, extremely tricky to handle. In his new design Wilhelm Maybach created a well-balanced car, the entire specification of which was more sophisticated than that of any other make. Fast, robust, easy to handle, it was named after *Mercédès Jellinek,* the daughter of the consul of Austria-Hungary at Nice, *Emil Jellinek,* who gave financial support for the successful model, which resulted in cars from the Daimler factory carrying the name Mercédès up to the time of the merger with Benz in 1926.

Mercédès, 1901, 4-cyl. 116 × 140 mm; 4⅝″ × 5½″, 35 hp

Mercédès "Simplex," 1902

Mercédès "Simplex," 1903

Mercédès, 1904, 18/28 HP

63

"28/60," 4-cyl., 1916

Sie fahren auf
**Ihre eigene Gefahr und Risiko
in diesem Wagen!**
ll.Vers.- Ges. v. 1.1.1926

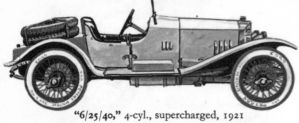

"6/25/40," 4-cyl., supercharged, 1921

"24/100/140,"
6-cyl., supercharged,
1924

The brass warning plate, fixed in front of the back seat in this 1916 model, had purely legal significance. It was in fact fitted to the car 10 years after it left the factory.

Even the complex supercharged models were robust designs, and were endowed with particularly fiery temperaments when Dr. Porsche took over in 1923. The "24/100/140" (German rating) began the legendary series of cars which culminated in 1931 in the "27/170/225 SSKL." The first number gives the fiscal hp, the second the effective hp without, and the third with, the supercharger—which produced an ear-splitting howl when the accelerator pedal was flat on the floor. Daimler's 1100 cc (67 cu. in.) V-2 engine (1½ hp) of 1899 provides a thought-provoking contrast with the six-times-larger supercharged unit in the 1927 "26/120/180" Mercedes-Benz (*left*).

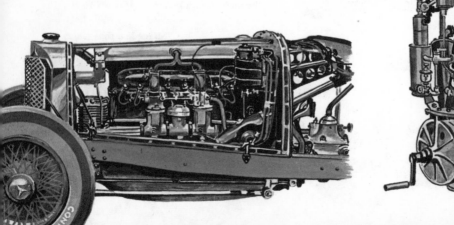

Benz, 1895, 8-seater Omnibus 1-cyl. (150 × 165 mm; 6″ × 6½″) motor at the rear. Chassis with belt transmission, chain-drive, and the classic Benz "Patent Motor Carriage" specification.

Benz retained his original model until 1901, with few modifications. The first 4-wheeled model appeared in 1891, and twin-cylinder motors were introduced in 1899, but the notorious belt transmission and complex controls lessened the popularity of the make. A new front-engined design, the "Elegant," was brought out in 1902 and the French engineer *Marius Barbarou* was then called in to design the "Parsifal" model. His work was taken over by *Hans Nibel,* who put the marque on the map with the "Blitzen-Benz," a racing car which set an absolute world record in 1909 at 125.95 mph.

When *Daimler-Benz AG* was established in 1926, the laurel wreath of the Benz emblem was placed around the Daimler star.

Benz "Spider," 1899

Benz, 1914, pointed radiator

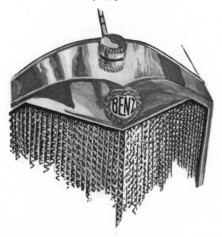

Benz "14/30," 1911

Benz "10/50," 1921

"Stuttgart 200," 1926

"Mannheim," 1926

"26/120/180 S," 1927

SS 1927

"27/170/225 SSK," 1928

SSK

SS 1928

The first *Mercedes-Benz*, the 2-liter 6-cyl. "8/38," bore the stamp of stagnating Benz design, despite its catalogue name of "Stuttgart 200," which referred to the Daimler factory. The "12/55" which appeared at the same time was, however, a direct descendant of the small Mercedes model, even though it was called the "Mannheim" as a friendly gesture toward the Benz factory, situated in that town. After extensive experiments with the 4- and 8-cyl. Mercedes racing cars of 1923, Dr. Porsche produced in 1925 the K sports model (33/140 hp). Its 6-liter engine underwent further development in the S, SS, and SSK series, finally becoming the SSKL (Super Sports Kurz Leicht) of 1931, with a 7.1-liter 6-cyl. motor (100 × 150 mm; 4″ × 6″). The individualistic Porsche had, however, left the works at the beginning of 1928.

The last Mercedes-Benz owned by ex-Kaiser Wilhelm II now stands in the firm's museum at Untertürkheim. It features a signaling system which allowed the Prussian ex-Emperor to give his driver orders without uttering one word. A row of buttons faced the Hohenzollern Prince in the back seat, marked *Left, Right, Fast, Slow, Turn around, Home,* and *Stop.* Pushing a button made a corresponding panel light up on the dashboard and the chauffeur could immediately carry out the Imperial command.

"27/170/225 SS," 1928

"300 SL," 1952

The numerous Mercedes-Benz models which have appeared since the 1930s reflect the make's characteristic combination of tradition with fresh technical inventiveness. Between the "170" of 1931, the firm's first automobile with independent rear suspension (swing axles), and the 1½-liter V-8 "W 165" racing car of 1939 with its two-stage supercharger, production encompassed straightforward family cars, sports cars, "status symbols" (in particular the "Grosser Mercedes" of 1937), formidable Grand Prix cars, and unusual rear-engined designs.

When production was started again in 1947 the only model was the "170 V," which was, however, soon joined by as wide a range of cars as before. In 1955 Mercedes won the World Championships for both sports cars (the Constructor's Championship) and GP cars (Driver's Championship—J. M. Fangio). There has always been an intensive and profitable relationship between the company's standard production models and their racing cars.

"220 SE," 1961

"Grosser Mercedes," 1937

"170 V," 1946

"130 H," 1934

"170 H," 1936

Using as a basis the "Teardrop-Benz" racing car of 1922 and the example set by Tatra, Daimler-Benz developed the 4-cyl. "130 H," with a backbone chassis and rear engine. It was followed two years later by the "170 H," with a 1.7-liter (104 cu.in.) engine.

67

FMR "KR 201"

The *FMR*—from Fahrzeug-und Maschinenbau GmbH, Regensburg—is better known as the *Messerschmitt* "Cabin Scooter," and was designed by two aircraft engineers, Messerschmitt and Fend. The three-wheeler KR 200 (closed) and KR 201 (open) models can reach 62 mph, while the four-wheeled "Tiger" does 80 mph. Tubular chassis with floor pan, rubber i.f.s., and a single-cyl. 2-cycle motor of 191 cc (Tiger: 2-cyl. 500 cc).

"Köln," 1938

The Ford Motor Company set up the *Deutsche Ford GmbH* company in 1925, and the following year built an assembly plant for the Model T (and later the A) in Berlin. Taking their cue from the world economic crisis, the European Ford works brought out in 1932 a small, cheap-to-run car, known in Britain as the "Model Y, 8 hp" (p. 122), in France as the "5 CV," and in Germany as the "Köln," to mark the factory's removal to Cologne in 1931. It had a 4-cyl. L-head motor of 933 cc (56.6 × 92.5 mm)—57 cu.in. (2¼″ × 3⅝″). These basically identical cars took on different characteristics; the bodywork of the "Köln" resembled the V-8s, and the "Eifel"—corresponding to the "10 hp" (p. 122)—was a further step toward a typically German car. The "Taunus" of 1939 was continued in 1948 with extra chrome until a fresh design, the "12M," came in 1952. The "17M" appeared in 1947 with the same front suspension as the "Consul" and a 1700 cc (104 cu.in.) valve-in-head motor. The interim "15M" had a similar 1½-liter engine and slightly altered bodywork.

In 1960 the Taunus design was completely reworked, and is now an amalgam of American, British, and German ideas.

"Eifel," 1939. The 2-passenger "Eifel" convertible was an anusually well-proportioned car; its 1172 cc (71.5 cu.in.) L-head motor was practically indestructible, and lent itself to further tuning. British enthusiasts obtained incredible outputs from the corresponding "Ten," although the standard brakes and steering needed suitable modification.

Ford V-8, 1938; Gläser bodywork

"Taunus," 1950

"Taunus," 1939

"12M," 1952

"17M," 1957

The Ford-Köln emblem uses the same script and oval motif as the parent factory in Dearborn to indicate the family relationship.

"17M," 1961

Germany

The boom in Germany during the 1950s killed the cruder minicars and created a demand for proper small cars that would be cheap to run.

Hans Glas GmbH, Isaria Maschinenfabrik, of Dingolfing, catered to this demand with its first car, the *Goggomobil,* launched in 1954 with a twin-cylinder 2-cycle motor mounted at the rear of a platform chassis. As economic conditions improved the bodywork became more stylish, and the specification changed to a 4-cyl. 4-cycle front-mounted engine in the S 1004.

Goggomobil, 1954

"TS 400," 1959

"Royal T 700," 1960

NSU (the name from the town of Neckarsulm) entered the cycle industry after having made knitting machines, and supplied the chassis for Daimler's Stahlradwagen (p. 63). This was followed by motorcycles and, from 1906-29, cars. Under license, Fiats were assembled here under the name, NSU-Fiat, changed in 1958 to *Neckar* when NSU resumed production of their own car designs. Recently NSU developed *Felix Wankel*'s epoch-making free piston engine, now interesting a number of manufacturers.

NSU, 1908

NSU-Wankel experimental engine, 1960

The carburetor and air filter of the Wankel engine take up more space than the engine proper

"Prinz," 1958
2-cyl. 600 cc (36.5 cu.in.) rear engine

"Sport-Prinz," 1960

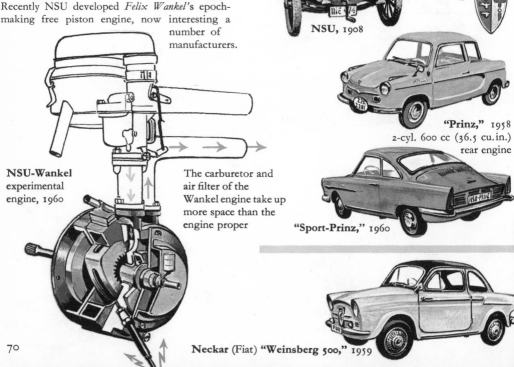

Neckar (Fiat) **"Weinsberg 500,"** 1959

Lutzmann, 1896

Friedrich Lutzmann, of Dessau, produced a substantial number of cars 1895-99, built on the "Lutzmann system," which was an improved and simplified version of the "Benz system," with steering and controls arranged far more conveniently. The firm sold both open and closed versions, for 2 to 8 passengers, and in 1896 built a 16-passenger bus.

Lutzmann, 1898

Opel-Darracq, 1902/03

When the old-established cycle works *Adam Opel AG,* of Rüsselsheim, was searching for a foothold in the infant German automobile industry around the start of the century, its first step was to acquire the "Lutzmann system." This type of vehicle was rapidly becoming obsolete, however, and in its place Opel obtained the agency for the French firm *Darracq,* then under British control. Opel built racing cars under Darracq license for the 1904 Gordon Bennett race, and before this assembled cars for sale under the name *Opel-Darracq.* A few years later, more original designs were developed, and the Darracq steering-column gear-shift was abandoned (only to be re-adopted some 40 years later). Up to 1914, through the whole of the inflationary period and the unsettled times which followed, the Opel factory survived as a family business, but was acquired in 1929 by *General Motors.*

Opel-Darracq, 1905

Opel, 1906

Opel "8/25," 1920. 4-cyl. magneto ignition, pressure lubrication and a self-starter.

Opel "10/18," 1908

Opel "4/8, Doctor's Car," 1909

Opel "6/16," 1910

Laubfrosch, "3/12," 1924

Opel "4/14," 1925

Sturdiness and a capacity for hard work were characteristic features of the Opel and made the marque extremely popular with customers who needed a completely reliable car, but could not afford to act as guinea pigs for bold technical experiments. The "Doctor's Car" of 1909 was a typical product of the practical attitude of the firm's directors, which later led to the "Laubfrosch" model (1924), a copy to the last detail of the *Citroën* "5CV" (p. 88).

Opel "4/14," 1928/29

With the 4-cyl. 1100 cc (67 cu.in.) model 4/14 Opel neared the end of independent existence. In competition with Ford, already well established in Germany, General Motors was looking for a factory which would allow them to manufacture cars in Europe. After GM had taken over the works at Rüsselsheim it was drastically reorganized for mass production, and trans-Atlantic ideas pervaded specifications, production, and marketing methods. The remodeled firm scored its first big success with the "Olympia" (4-cyl. 1300 cc; 80 cu.in.) which was launched at the time of the Berlin Olympic Games in 1936. This was joined by the "Six" and "Super-Six" series, which in 1939 grew into the 6-cyl. 2½-liter (151 cu.in.) "Kapitän." The smallest model in the range was named the "Kadett," and at the top of the range was the "Admiral" with a 79 bhp 6-cyl. engine. The Olympia became the "Rekord," which has been produced over a number of years in many different forms.

"Olympia," 1936

"Olympia," 1950

"Super Six," 1938

"Kapitän," 1960

"Kapitän," 1939

"Rekord," 1961

"Admiral," 1938

VW "Berlin-Rome"

PORSCHE

1948 Prototype

"356," 1954

The germ of the idea for the cars coming today from the *Dr. Ing. h. c. F. Porsche KG* factory at Stuttgart-Zuffenhausen can be seen in early designs by Dr. Ferdinand Porsche for *Zündapp* and *NSU* and in the racing "P-Wagen" built by *Auto Union* to his design. This work was followed by the "Kraft durch Freude" car—better known as the *Volkswagen*. A more specific starting-point, however, would be the modified VW which was built in the winter of 1938/39, with a special streamlined body, for the Berlin-Rome Long-Distance Rally. After the defeat of the Berlin-Rome Axis, Porsche worked in Austria where, as a purely private venture, his son *Ferry Porsche* carried out a conversion of the VW so far-reaching that a new make resulted and was given the Porsche design number 356. The first production model, with closed bodywork, was shown at Geneva in 1949 and created such a demand that the firm was obliged to move to its present factory in Stuttgart.

"1500 Super"
4-cyl. 1488 cc
(91 cu. in.)
rear engine
(80 × 74 mm;
3⅛″ × 3″)
70 bhp
at 5000 rpm

The air-cooled horizontally opposed layout is all that remains from the VW motor. 25 bhp was increased to 40 in 1948 and to 102 bhp in the 365B/1600S-90 model.

"1600 Super," 1961, 90 bhp

The original **KDF** prototype
of 1938 became the Volkswagen

1939-53
Divided rear window
Single exhaust pipe

1953-57
One-piece rear window
1955 twin exhaust pipes

1957
Larger rear window
1960 Blinkers
1962 Gasoline gauge

The Volkswagen is at once a worthy memorial to Dr. Porsche's contribution to European automobile engineering, and a striking example of the importance of sales and service in the marketing of an automobile. The make's unique position throughout the world must be attributed to fundamentally robust design and astute marketing technique, coupled with constant development of the basic design. The unpretentious body style has been kept without any striking modifications. From 985 cc—60 cu. in. (70×64 mm; $2\frac{3}{4}'' \times 2\frac{1}{2}''$) in 1939-48 the engine has been enlarged to 1131 cc —69 cu. in. (75×64 mm; $3'' \times 2\frac{1}{2}''$) and again to 1192 cc—72.7 cu. in. (77×64 mm; $3\frac{1}{8}'' \times 2\frac{1}{2}''$) in 1954. The crash gearbox was replaced by synchromesh in 1952; hydraulic brakes were offered on de luxe models in 1950 and increased in size in 1958. The springs, shock absorbers, internal trim, rear lights and so on have changed with time—but Dr. Porsche's basic idea of a compact, economical means of transport is still paramount, even in the "1500" (83×69 mm; $3\frac{1}{4}'' \times 2\frac{3}{4}''$) brought out in 1961.

"1500," 1961

Germany

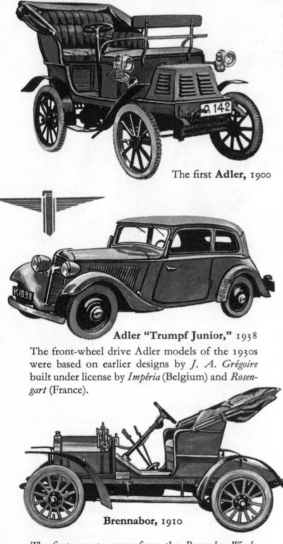

The first **Adler,** 1900

Heinrich Kleyer added single-cylinder De Dion Bouton cars to his production of *Adler* bicycles in 1900, and later developed his own car designs and a flourishing motorcycle business. Automobile manufacture was not resumed after 1945.

Adler, 1913-14

Adler "Trumpf Junior," 1938

The front-wheel drive Adler models of the 1930s were based on earlier designs by *J. A. Grégoire* built under license by *Impéria* (Belgium) and *Rosengart* (France).

The "Champion" was a modern variation on the "people's car" theme which has always been popular in Germany. It had a backbone chassis, with a 2-cyl. 2-cycle ILO rear engine (398 cc; 24 cu.in.) delivering 14 bhp. Rubber suspension and many other chassis details were ahead of their time, but the car failed to meet the demand for more performance which came with the postwar boom.

"Champion,"
1952

Brennabor, 1910

The first cars to come from the *Brennabor-Werke* cycle factory of the *Reichstein* brothers were light "people's cars"; the firm did not survive the aftermath of the inflation years.

One of the BMW forerunners from the *Fahrzeugfabrik Eisenach* was the Dixi. This make, too, was unsuited to conditions during the inflation period, and the firm turned to license production of the Austin "Seven."

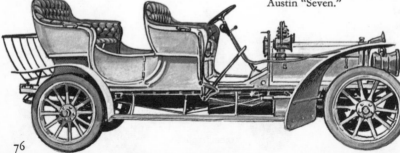

Dixi, 1906
4-cyl. 4900 cc
(299 cu.in.)

Dürkopp, 1901
2-cyl. 8 hp

This factory made sewing machines and, later, cars on the Panhard & Levassor "system." The make lasted until 1928.

Gutbrod "Superior," 1952. Another of the ephemeral "people's cars" of the 1950s. It was technically interesting, having a 2-cycle fuel-injection motor. Relatively high performance: 27 bhp and 68 mph.

Hanomag, 1938

The *Hannoversche Maschinenbau AG* entered the German car industry in 1914, although the name did not become famous until the "Kommissbrot" model of 1925. This car was reduced to the bare essentials needed for carrying two people. The models of the 1930s were more conventional, but gradually acquired very streamlined bodywork, and later versions were available with Diesel engines. Car production never regained its footing after 1945 in spite of the promising front-wheel drive "Partner" with its 3-cyl. 2-cycle engine.

"Kommissbrot," 1925

"As only tin and paint is used, the Hanomag is soon produced," ran an unkind contemporary doggerel about the single-cylinder rear-engined "Kommissbrot," i.e. "Quartermaster's Loaf."

"Partner," 1952

Front-wheel drive by a 2-cycle 3-cyl. engine (65×70 mm, 697 cc; $2\frac{5}{8}'' \times 2\frac{3}{4}''$, 42.5 cu.in.) giving 28 bhp. The car was too heavy for the motor, weighing over $\frac{3}{4}$ ton.

Maico "500," 1957

The twin-cylinder 2-cycle Maico was made by the motorcycle and scooter firm, but abandoned due to financial problems.

Kleinschnittger "FN 25," 1951
One of the postwar baby cars which did not survive.

In automotive history the sublime is seldom far from the ridiculous; a great deal depends upon the purpose of the design and the attitude of the designer. A *Maybach* was built regardless of economic considerations, while a *Phänomobil* was clearly closely related to the motorcycle. Each in its own way made contributions to automotive development, and their basic concepts constantly recur.

Maybach, 1933

Vilhelm Maybach came to the Zeppelin works from Daimler, and started producing cars in 1921 with a 6-cyl. 6-liter model. This was followed in 1929 by a handsome V-12 (8-liter; 490 cu in.) giving over 200 bhp at 2800 rpm. Despite their size and weight the cars were fast and handled well, and were particularly well suited to custom-built coachwork. The price was astronomical.

Phänomobil, 1911

With a twin-cylinder motor mounted over the front wheel, this vehicle from the *Phänomenwerke* provided minimum, reliable transport. It was also available with 4 seats and, after 1912, with 4 cylinders. Top speed about 40 mph.

Veritas, 1950

After 1947 a group of BMW engineers tried to establish the *Veritas,* on the basis of 1939 BMW designs. They entered into collaboration in 1950 with Panhard & Levassor, whose 2-cyl. Dyna motor was used in the Dyna-Veritas. The make was absorbed by BMW when they started up again.

Piccolo-Mobbel, 1909
1 cyl. 649 cc (39 cu. in.)

Zündapp's unorthodox symmetrical "Janus" (1 cyl. 2-cycle 248 cc [15 cu. in.] engine under the central seat) never went into series production.

Stoewer, 1910

The *Stoewer* Brothers of Stettin were responsible for some unorthodox designs, but the make disappeared during the late 1930s.

Zündapp "Janus," 1956

When the Iron Curtain split Germany into East and West, Auto Union (Audi, DKW, Horch, and Wanderer) and BMW were cut off from West Germany. Cars of East German registration still carry the "D" nationality plate. East Germany produces about 75,000 units a year.

EMW "340/2," 1949

Using the initials of the *Eisenacher Motoren Werke* and BMW mechanical components in a slightly altered bodywork, the original BMW works tried to live up to their old renown and compete with the West German company.

EMW "327," 1952

The sports model "327" was also made in East Germany. From 1953 the "340" was slightly changed in specification and appearance and given the designation "340/8." Eisenach cars bore the old BMW emblem, but with red enamel and the new initials.

EMW "340/8," 1952

The "people's factory" at Zwickau, where Horch had built their cars, produced a prototype "P50" (2-cyl. 500 cc [30.5 cu. in.] two-cycle) in 1957; this came on the market in 1959 as the *Trabant* (Satellite). It resembles early DKW models.

DKW and BMW found new life west of the Iron Curtain although production continued in the original factories under different names. Audi and Wanderer did not reappear, and Horch has been seen only sporadically as *Sachsenring*.

IFA "F9," 1951

In the old Audi factory the *Industrievereinigung, Fahrzeugbau* built a copy of DKW's 3-cyl. 1939 model. The original was made at Ingolstadt, West Germany, after 1960 by Daimler-Benz.

Wartburg "311," 1960

An old name was brought back into circulation when the IFA was renamed the "Wartburg." This name had been used early in the century by the forerunners of the BMW.

Trabant, 1960

Denmark

The history of the Danish automotive industry reflects developments in other small countries. Pioneers with original ideas, imagination, and a belief in the future of the motorcar showed remarkable technical and commercial initiative, but were hampered by reactionary attitudes and political narrow-mindedness. Nevertheless

Denmark's most precious automobile treasure, the *Hammel,* traditionally dated at 1886/87 but perhaps younger, is owned by the Technical Museum. It was carefully and thoroughly restored by F. Bülow & Co., and in 1954 it completed the 56½-mile London-to-Brighton Run in 12 hr 47 min.

a native industry was in the making while the building of cars was still at the stage between craftsmanship and industrial production, but only one factory, *Triangel,* produced in appreciable quantity. In the end even this one could not compete with the industrial might of the bigger countries, whose assembly plants today produce the only cars built in Denmark. Subsequent attempts to create a Danish car industry have all been defeated because of a lack of technical potential and insufficient capital for large production. In any case large-scale production could not be expected, since the home market is limited and subject to keen competition from the world's main manufacturers, while export prospects would be limited.

The vehicle was built by A. F. Hammel and H. U. Johansen, with a horizontal twin-cylinder motor (104.5 × 160 mm, 2720 cc; 4⅛″ × 6¼″, 165 cu.in.) giving 3½ hp at 400 rpm. Water-cooling, surface carburetor, reverse gear driving from the camshaft, and chain drive to the rear wheels.

Hammel, 1886/87 (?)
completed the London-Brighton Run in 1954.

Brems, 1900

In 1899-1900 A. L. Brems, a machinery manufacturer of Viborg, built a single-cylinder air-cooled engine car closely modeled on the German Wartburg (pp. 58 & 79). Eight cars were produced.

While Brems very quickly gave up the idea of making cars, H. C. Christiansen established the *Dansk Automobil- og Cyclefabrik, H.C. Christiansen & Co.* The firm was the first real Danish car factory, and concentrated on buses and taxis. Christiansen supplied the first taxi registered in Copenhagen in 1903, K 800. It had a single-cylinder engine.

Dansk Automobil- og Cyclefabrik, 1903

H. C. Christiansen ran a cycle works in Copenhagen from 1896 on, where he produced a prototype light car about 1899. His partner, Fonnesbech-Wulff had grandiose schemes, and in 1904 founded the *Dansk Automobilselskab A/S* in connection with the factory. This company was to run a network of car services all over Denmark; test routes were successfully run, and despite the meager capital the scheme seemed promising. When the Danish parliament passed a law prohibiting night driving, however, it became impossible to carry out the plans. The company was liquidated, and as the factory was near collapse, in 1906 it switched to the import business.

The 1899 prototype belongs to the Technical Museum. It has a tubular chassis typical of its period, a single-cylinder water-cooled motor with automatic inlet valve, friction transmission, and chain-drive to the rear axle.

Christiansen, 1899

Denmark

Anglo-Dane, 1902

In spite of its English-sounding name, the first car made by *H. C. Frederiksen* was inspired by a German design, the *Maurer-Union,* and employed that make's friction transmission. Anglo-Dane cars found a fairly wide market, and in 1904 production of motorcycles bearing the same name was begun. Restrictions on driving after 1914 threatened to ruin the firm, and it ceased to be an independent entity when Th. B. Thrige brought about the merger of Anglo-Dane, JAN, and Thrige to form *De Forenede Automobilfabriker A/S* in 1918. The new company built only Thrige designs, and the cars thereafter bore the *Triangel* trademark.

JAN, 1915

Around 1914 *Jan Hagemeister* built cars to which he gave his own Christian name. Wartime restrictions closed the factory, but not before Hagemeister had designed a 6-cyl. 75 hp engine in 1916 which anticipated the BMW 327/28 layout of 1936. In 1913 he applied for a patent on a gas turbine.

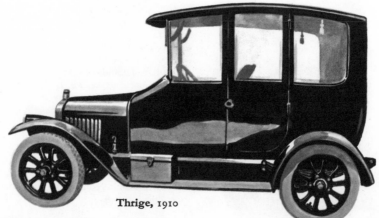

Thrige, 1910

Thomas B. Thrige, whose life's work was a large engineering firm at Odense, took a keen interest in the possibilities of the motorcar industry and built an experimental car in 1909. The following year series-production of the Thrige cars was begun; these achieved substantial home sales before the fusion with JAN and Anglo-Dane.

After the merger, the "United Automobile Factories" gave up passenger-car production to devote their energies to trucks, buses, and locomotives. A large proportion of the components were made in Odense, including a 4-cyl. 50 bhp motor with aluminum pistons in 1923. Otherwise *Ballot, White & Poppe, Continental,* and *Hercules* engines were used. As time went by Triangel vehicles became far more of an assembled product, and after 1945 the firm's activities were directed solely to importing. DFA had already represented *Austin* since 1931 (and previously *FN, Fiat,* and *Studebaker*); only the word "United" remains to recall Thomas B. Thrige's great contribution to the Danish car industry.

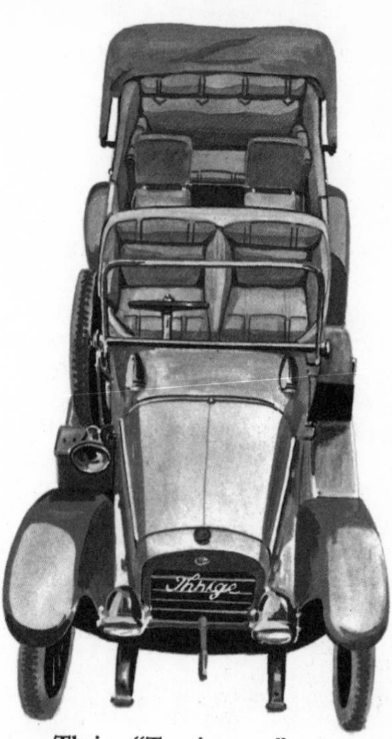

The first Thrige cars shone in Danish reliability trials, and the factory did not forget its sporting background when production was restricted to heavy chassis. A standard bus chassis fitted with an open two-seater body finished second in the 1927 Danish race from Rome to Copenhagen.

Thrige "Touring car," 1914

Triangel "Rome-Copenhagen," 1927

Spain's car industry is as paradoxical as Cervantes' Don Quixote. While ignoring elementary personal transport needs, Spanish factories have produced exclusive, costly, and exotic cars which occupy a place of honor in the crowded museum of motoring rarities—vehicles like the *Elizalde* and the *Nacional-Pescara*. Recent years have seen growing production under foreign license.

The first *Hispano-Suiza* of 1904 was an example of Birkigt's clear-cut designs.

The Hispano-Suiza emblem symbolizes the union of Spanish capital and Swiss engineering know-how in 1904, when the young railway engineer *Marc Birkigt* designed the first of these famous cars for Spanish interests; from 1911 onward they were also built in France.

Racing car, 1910. The 4 cylinders (65×200 mm—originally 140; $2\frac{5}{8}'' \times 7\frac{7}{8}''$—$5\frac{1}{2}''$) were cast *en bloc*. This model won the 1910 Coupe des Voiturettes.

All early Hispano-Suizas had side-valve engines with inlet and exhaust valves on opposite sides of the block (T-head layout). The marque won the special attention of King Alfonso XIII, and on the basis of the Coupe model the legendary sports model "15 T" was developed.

This was made from 1911 (4-cyl. 80×180 mm, 3604 cc; $3\frac{1}{8}'' \times 7\frac{1}{8}''$, 220 cu.in.) and was the first to come from the French subsidiary factory.

"20/24" (4-cyl. 3758 cc, 100×120 mm; 229 cu.in., $4'' \times 4\frac{3}{4}''$), 1906, was an attractive, well-thought-out design, with gearbox and crank-case in one unit.

The "15T" became known as the "Alfonso" model. It combined performance and excellent handling with a silken gearshift (3-speed transmission during the first years, 4-speed later) and sensitive, precise steering. The car laid the foundation for the make's well-merited fame. The mechanical specification and finish were perfection itself, so much so in later models that Rolls-Royce, for instance, used Hispano-Suiza wheel mountings under license.

Hispano-Suiza "15T"

"15T Alfonso XIII," 1912

Birkigt, who as early as 1912 was working on a supercharged engine, designed a V-8 aero-engine with overhead valves and an overhead camshaft for each cylinder block. This was used in 1914-18 by the Allied air forces, and produced in Britain, France, and the USA. It was fitted in the French Spad fighters used by famous ace Georges Guynemer and his squadron. Using the stork of Lorraine as their emblem, symbolizing the fight to regain the lost border province, the squadron was feared all along the Western Front. After 1918 Hispano-Suiza took over the stork as a radiator mascot, even for automobiles made at Barcelona.

La Cigogne Volante

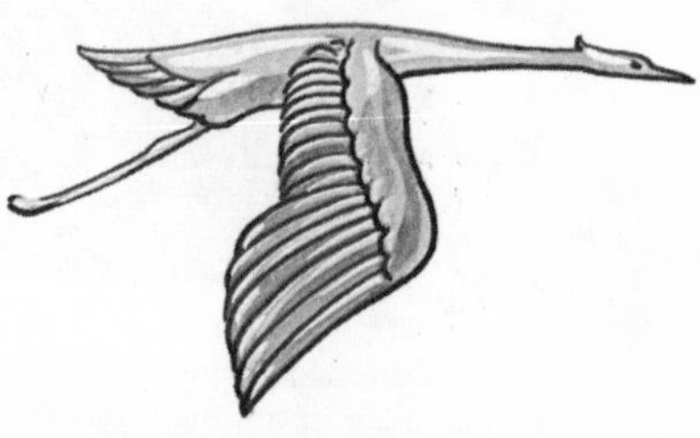

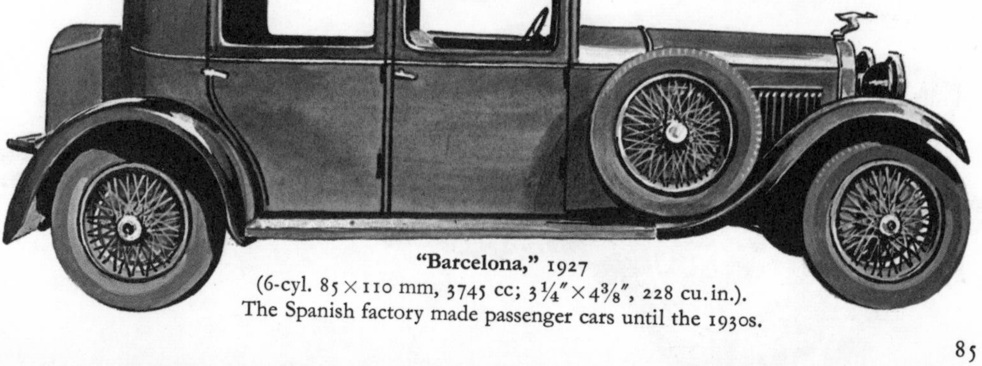

"Barcelona," 1927
(6-cyl. 85 × 110 mm, 3745 cc; 3¼″ × 4⅜″, 228 cu. in.).
The Spanish factory made passenger cars until the 1930s.

Pegaso "102"
1951, factory bodywork

If the Hispano-Suiza recalls Don Quixote, then this is even truer of the *Pegaso*, brought out in 1951 by *Empresa Nacional de Autocamiones SA*, who had taken over Hispano-Suiza. From its name ENASA might be thought to be aimed at supplying Spain with sorely needed trucks—but the factory also produced a fabulous car designed by *Wilfredo P. Ricart*, previously of Alfa-Romeo.

"Z 102" engine

The engine was a V-8 which, in the Z-models, had 4 overhead camshafts. The "Z 102" was of 2.5 or 2.8 liters, the later "Z 103" of 4½ liters. A 3.2-liter model was also built and, with special body, exceeded 150 mph. The chassis was a stout platform with welded cross-members and wheel arches, and the bodies were made either by the factory or by custom coach builders. Production ceased in 1958.

5-speed transmission behind a limited-slip differential; torsion-bar springing, inboard brakes, and a De Dion axle.

Two-seater chassis

86

Pegaso "Z 102," 1953
"Thrill Berlinetta" by Carrozeria Touring,
Milan, certainly lived up to its name. Lavish in its
engineering and bodywork, exceedingly fast, and
highly expensive.

With the open, factory bodywork a
Pegaso "Z 102" was good for about
155 mph. The make was entered for
Le Mans in 1952, but did not compete.

Spanish license manufacture covers a range of current British, French,
Italian, and German models, the most important being SEAT, a
Spanish Fiat. The little Autonacional is a Voisin design.

Autonacional "Biscuter 200 R," 1957

SEAT "500"
one of the Fiat models from *Sociedad
Española de Automoviles de Turismo.*

"200 F," 1960

The first mechanical vehicle of usable size was built by a Frenchman; the first four-wheeled gasoline-engined car not to bear the stamp of the horse-drawn carriage was built by a French firm. It was in France that the automobile took shape, and there the automobile industry was born. Bold initiative, a great deal of mechanical skill and sound business sense gave the French industry a dominance which, through license agreements, spread far beyond her own frontiers. Competition increased after the turn of the century, but between 1920 and 1939 French cars continued to set the standards, and fashions in car styling were dictated by French coach-building firms. The 1929–30 crisis brought the first disquieting tremors, and these spread to bring down some technically brilliant but financially less stable makes. After 1945 the last of the proud names, cars which could justifiably bear the title "Grandes Voitures," slowly disappeared. This was due in part to discriminatory legislation, but also to a financial climate which favored concentration of production on the smaller type of car. The annual production of cars in France runs at about 1,300,000 units.

Andre Citroën began his career in 1913 making double helical gears. As an industrialist he was keenly interested in the possibilities of mass production, and particularly of modern factory methods in a large-scale car industry. He was not himself an automobile engineer, but he commissioned *Jules Salomon* to design a car which would be both sturdy and suitable for large-series production. The result was the "Type A" which, while it had no pretensions to beauty, was an almost indestructible piece of engineering. Fitted with a 4 cyl. engine (65 × 100 mm, 1327 cc; $2\frac{5}{8}'' \times 4''$, 80 cu.in.), more than 10,000 were made each year from 1919-21.

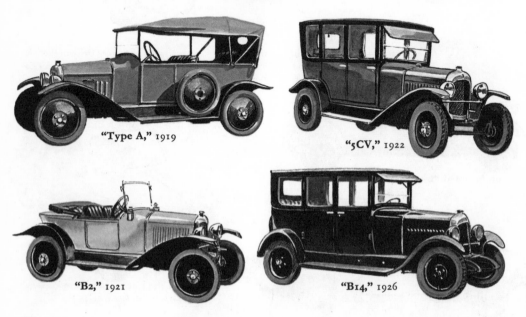

"Type A," 1919

"5CV," 1922

"B2," 1921

"B14," 1926

Confidence in the ability of the motorcar to solve any land-transport problem lay behind the design of the *Citroën-Kegresse* half-track models. In 1923 *Georges-Marie Haardt* and *Louis Audouin-Dubreuil* crossed the Sahara from north to south. The following years, a convoy of white-painted Citroën-Kegresse cars traveled from Colomb-Bechar across the Sahara to the Chad, and then on southward across French Equatorial Africa to Mozambique, which was reached on

Citroën-Kegresse, 1928-29

June 14, 1925. A third expedition was made in 1931-32 from Beirut to Peking, and took the vehicles over the Himalayas. Civilian use of the Kegresse models was mainly in agriculture, while the Army used them as transport in difficult terrain.

"C 6," 1928

"10 HP," 1933

In the "B 12" series of 1925 Citroën introduced four-wheel brakes and mass-produced steel bodies. In 1926 the "B14" got an improved engine, and subsidiary companies were established in England and Belgium. The "C4" and "C6" of 1928 were a considerable advance, and "Rosalie II" (C6) and "La Petite Rosalie" (C4) set class records in 1932 and 1933 with 130,000 km in 54 days (64.6 mph) and 300,000 km in 134 days (57.8 mph).

The Citroën "7A" which was presented to the public on April 15, 1934, was a clean break with the past. Front-wheel drive, torsion-bar suspension, and an integral body shell with unusual lines were all in themselves remarkable features; together they added up to a revolution in design.

"11CV Normale," 1938

The model "7A" became, in 1935, the "11CV Normale" and "11CV Légere"— 4-cyl. types which stayed in production until 1957. The 6-cyl. "15CV" was announced in 1938.

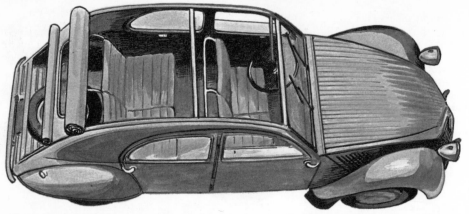

Citroën engineers had been working on the plans for a small, economy car since the middle 1930s. The war brought development to a standstill, but in 1948 the factory came out with the **"2CV,"** which was just as revolutionary in appearance and engineering as the "7 A" had been 14 years earlier. A twin-cylinder air-cooled engine (62×62 mm, 375 cc; $2\frac{3}{8}'' \times 2\frac{3}{8}''$, 22.9 cu.in.) delivered 9 bhp to the front wheels, whose suspension was linked to the rear wheels on each side.

"DS 19," 1955

"ID 19," 1956

The two chevrons are derived from Citroën's first emblem, and represent the double helical gears manufactured by André Citroën from 1913 onward.

The "DS 19" of 1955 was an outstanding innovation. Adjustable pneumatic suspension, self-compensated braking, servo steering, gear-shifting and clutch action—all from a central hydraulic system. The "ID 19" appeared in 1956 with the same suspension, but with non-automatic clutch, gearshift, steering, and brakes. Both models have disc brakes at the front and drums at the rear.

"DS19" convertible, 1960

DB

DB, 1954, with Chausson fiberglass body, 850 cc (51.8 cu.in.) Panhard motor with low-pressure supercharger.

Charles Deutsch and *René Bonnet* built their first **DB,** based on a Citroën "Traction Avant," in 1936 (*above*). After 1945 they used the Panhard & Levassor "Dyna" engine and DB's extremely efficient sports cars with this power unit have had convincing Index wins in the Le Mans 24-Hour Race (including 1959-60-61). The partnership broke up early in 1962.

DB 850 cc (51.8 cu.in.), 1960

Facellia, 1650 cc (100 cu.in.), 1960

Facel "Vega," 1954

The coach-building firm of *Facel S.A.* built a chassis in 1954, fitted it with the Chrysler V-8 motor, and called the resulting car the "Vega." Gradually it developed into a sporting and distinguished-looking car, and in 1960 the smaller "Facellia" was introduced with the firm's own motor, and now uses the *Volvo* motor.

Facel-Vega "Excellence," 1956 "HK 500," 1960

Facellia, 1961

91

France

Prototype
1889/90

Emile Levassor's place of honor in motoring history is due to his realization that the Daimler engine was suitable for use in a car, and to his revolutionary layout of the main design components, with the engine at the front followed by a gearbox driving the rear wheels via chains. Between his prototype of 1889/90 and the "Système Panhard & Levassor" of 1890/91 lies the dividing line between the horse-drawn carriage and the motorcar. There was sound good sense behind Levassor's design; the weight of the motor gave the steering front wheels a better grip of the road—something much to be desired as the roads were often soft, and the wheels hard. A gearbox was noisier but far more reliable than belt transmission. The tiller was replaced by a wheel and gear-mechanism in 1898, removing the weakest feature of the original design. The make kept its technical lead for some ten years, but remained highly respected and later showed a refreshing technical freedom of thought.

"Système Panhard & Levassor," 1890/91

"16CV," 1901

The factory departed from its proven "système" in 1902 to build this *Denis de Boisse* model, which was quickly dropped.

"20CV," 1913
Labourdette body

"X19," 1912, 4-cyl. (70 × 140, 2150 cc; 2¾″ × 5½″, 131 cu.in.), built as a light model.

92

8-cyl. **"35CV,"** 1925

"6DS," 1930, 6-cyl.

The patents taken out by the English-born American *Charles Yale Knight* in 1905 and 1908 for a motor with double sleeves instead of the normal valves were used by a number of leading European makes: Daimler, Minerva, Siddeley-Deasy, Rover, Mercedes and, from 1909, Panhard & Levassor. After 1920 production was concentrated on these types, of which the 6.3-liter "35CV" was the largest.

Panhard & Levassor's last model with standard valves left the works in 1922. Before this only the sleeve-valve models bore the letters SS on the radiator as an indication that they were "Sans Soupapes" (valveless) in the current sense of the word. It was not until the "Dyna" series that the factory again made "valve engines." The distinctive "Dynamic," which was made from 1936, had a sleeve-valve engine with aerodynamic, stressed bodywork on a tubular backbone chassis, partly enclosed wheels, and a centrally placed driving seat. The "Dyna," which appeared at the 1946 Paris Salon with a 610 cc—38 cu. in. (72×75 mm; 2⅞"×3") engine, was created by *J. A. Grégoire*. The preliminary studies and early constructional experiments had been completed during the German occupation, so that the factory was able to put the model into production very quickly. Since 1955 the firm has formed part of the Citroën concern.

"Dynamic," 1936   **"Dyna,"** 1948

After 1945 the factory made only the "Dyna" model with a 2-cyl. air-cooled engine, front-wheel drive, and lightweight body. It had an advanced specification while being typical of its time. The "Dyna"

engine was increased to 850 cc (52 cu. in.) and to 1000 cc (60 cu. in.) in a sports version. The body styling was changed in 1954, with further modification as the "PL 17" of 1959.

"PL 17," 1960

"PL 5," 1945

France

"3.5CV," 1891

"8CV," 1900

"5CV," 1903

This popular "voiturette," with a single-cylinder engine, was quite clearly influenced by De Dion-Bouton's similar models.

"Bebe," 1913
4-cyl. 55 × 90 mm
856 cc (2¼″ × 3⅝″,
52.8 cu. in.)

T-head Bugatti design, built under license by Peugeot 1912-14.

Lion-Peugeot, 1908/09

The forebears of *Armand Peugeot* had manufactured hardware in France since the days of the French Revolution, and the bicycle factory he set up in 1885 formed part of the family business, *Les Fils de Peugeot Frères*. The first Peugeot was a quadricycle with a 2-cyl. Daimler motor, supplied by Panhard & Levassor. After 1896 Peugeot built their own engines designed by *Rigoulot,* and in the following year established the *Société des Automobiles Peugeot*. The rear-engine design was abandoned after 1900 —one of the last was supplied to the King of Sweden—and at the same time the family firm began to compete with automobiles called *Lion-Peugeot*. In 1908 the two firms were combined in *S. A. des Automobiles Peugeot*.

"Quadrilette," 1921

"18CV," 1925

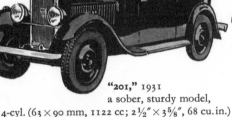

"201," 1931
a sober, sturdy model,
4-cyl. (63 × 90 mm, 1122 cc; 2½″ × 3⅝″, 68 cu.in.)
s.v.

"301," 1934

"402," 1936, with retractable hard-top

The "402" of 1935 was of striking appearance, with a sound mechanical specification. An excellent 1.9-liter valve-in-head 4-cyl. motor was a better sales argument than the modernistic body, but the model remained in production in various forms until replaced by the "203" in 1948. The "203" motor featured hemispherical combustion chambers with inclined o.h. valves. The same layout was used by *Ernest Henry* for the marque's racing car of 1912, although with 4 valves per cylinder and two o.h. camshafts.

The "203" of 1948 was in production through 1960, when the 1290 cc—78.6 cu.in. (75 × 73 mm; 3″ × 2⅞″) motor was transferred to the "403" body.

The "403" of 1955 (4-cyl. 1468 cc, 80 × 73 mm; 89.5 cu.in., 3⅛″ × 2⅞″) was based on the "203." 1960 saw the "404," also with a body by *Pininfarina,* the bore increased to 84 mm, and modified front suspension.

Renault, 1904, 2-cyl.

"1.75CV," 1898, 1-cyl. De Dion motor

2-cyl., 1910

"35CV," 1912, 6-cyl.

The three *Renault* brothers entered the infant French motorcar industry with all the enthusiasm of their youth, and the financial backing of a compliant father. *Louis* was the technical master-mind of the three, and was assisted by *Marcel* as works driver until his death in the 1903 Paris-Madrid Race. *Fernand* died after an illness 1909. From the very first models the engine was placed at the front, driving the rear wheels via a gearbox and cardan shaft at a time when chain drive was more usual. From being a hobby their car-building grew into an industry, and in 1902 they gave up using De Dion engines and made their own 4-cyl. types. They had numerous racing successes, and the historic movement of troops to the Marne in 1914 was carried out in Renault taxis.

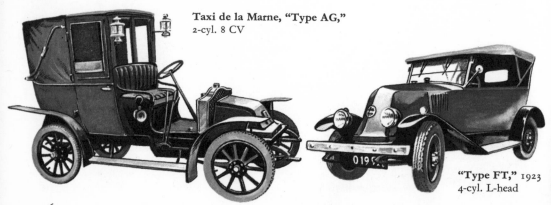

Taxi de la Marne, "Type AG,"
2-cyl. 8 CV

"Type FT," 1923
4-cyl. L-head

In 1923-27 the "40CV" (45HP) was Renault's most distinguished model; 6-cyl. (110×160 mm, 9200 cc; 4⅜″×6¼″, 562 cu.in.).

Fitted with a light, 4-seater open body a "40CV" Renault set a world 24-hour speed record in 1925 at 87.6 mph, and in the following year, with a closed body, raised it to 107.8 mph.

"Celtaquatre," 1935
4-cyl. 1463 cc (89 cu.in.)

"Viva Grand Sport," 1938. This developed further the body styling produced by bringing the radiator to the front in 1929.

"4CV," 1948

A small rear-engined model was prepared during the German occupation, and exhibited at the 1946 Salon as the "R1060," better known as the "4CV" (in Britain as the Renault 750). Water-cooled 750 cc (45.6 cu.in.) 4-cyl. engine (54.5×80 mm; 2⅛″ ×3⅛″). Series-production began in 1948.

From the very first, Renault cars were notable for a clean and clear layout of components. To save the engine from being covered in road dirt, the radiator was first placed along the closed sides of the hood, and then at the rear of the engine compartment. Between 1929 and 1946 the layout was more orthodox. After the liberation Louis Renault, accused of collaboration, died in prison. The Billancourt works were nationalized. The "Frégate" series was introduced in 1951 (4-cyl. 85×88 mm, 1997 cc [3¼″×3½″, 122 cu.in.] front engine), followed by the "Dauphine" (4-cyl. 58×80 mm, 845 cc [2¼″×3⅛″, 51.6 cu.in.] rear engine) in 1956,with the "Floride" variant (*Pietro Frua* body design) in 1959. A front-wheel drive "R 4" with a "4CV" engine came out in 1961.

left : **"Frégate,"** 1951
center : **"Dauphine,"** 1957
right : **"Floride,"** 1959

France

Some cars result from an engineer's creative urge, others from purely commercial considerations. A very few are the result of a happy combination of the two motives. *Simca*'s history can be traced back to *Henri Theodor Pigozzi*'s activities as an importer of cars from his native Italy. As economic restrictions after the 1929 crisis made this difficult, Pigozzi took up assembly production of *Fiat*'s "Balilla" model in 1932 and marketed it as the *Fiat Française*. Two years later he acquired a larger works, and the *Société Industrielle de Mécanique et Carosserie Automobile* was established.

"Huit," 1951
4-cyl. 72×75 mm, 1221 cc
(2⅞″×3″, 74.5 cu.in.);
the Fiat "Nuova Balilla 1100"
in slightly altered form.

1) Fiat Française, 1932 (Fiat "508 Balilla")
2) Simca-Fiat, 1934 (Fiat "508 Balilla")
3) Simca-Fiat "Onze," 1935 (Fiat "518 Ardita")
4) Simca "Huit," 1937 (Fiat "508 C Nuova Balilla")

Using the new company's initials as an insignia, Simca steadily increased their production and absorbed a number of older, French makes: *Donnet-Zedel,* which was bought out in 1934, was made up of two older makes which had earlier been taken over by *Vinot-Deguingand.* The French *Ford* works was acquired in 1954; *Talbot* and *Unic* have also become part of Simca. In 1948 the company introduced a technical design of its own with the "Neuf," and in 1951 the first in the "Aronde" series.

"Cinq," 1937
alias the Fiat "500 Topolino";
the first to carry the Simca
name without suffix.

"1200 Sport," 1950

"Six," 1949

Amédée Gordini exploited the great potential of the "1100" engine in sports and racing cars.

"Neuf," 1951
"Aronde"

Simca-Gordini, 1950

"Ariane," 1961   "Etoile Six," 1961

Aronde body+Aronde engine=Aronde.
Ford "Vedette" body+Aronde engine=Ariane.
Vedette body+Ford V-8 engine=Vedette.

Donnet "4CV," 1931
2-cycle 2-cyl. (79×75 mm, 740 cc;
3⅛″×3″, 45 cu. in.)
designed by Violet.

Georges Richard was, in his own way, the forerunner of Pigozzi. He began with cars modeled on the *Benz,* then built the *Vivinus* under license and joined up with *Henri Brasier,* who had been a mechanic and driver with *Mors.* Together they developed the *Richard-Brasier.* Brasier later worked on his own account.

Unic "Double Phaeton," 1908

This make was a typical example of sound but not particularly inspired French engineering; it had its origins in Georges Richard's dream of conquering the market with a single model, hence the name.

The *Ateliers de Construction de Motocycles et Accessoires* is a French subsidiary of the Italian *Piaggio* factory which makes the Vespa scooters. From 1957-61 the French concern built a 2-cycle 2-cyl. rear-engined *Vespa* car, based on an Italian prototype.

Georges Richard, 1903, 2-cyl. 10HP   **Vespa "400,"** 1957

France

Ader "8CV," 1902
2-cyl. Double Phaeton

The makes to be found in the wrecking yard of the French industry range from the magnificent to the comic. *Clément Ader* was better known as a telephone engineer, although an insatiable urge to invent led him to experiment with a steam aircraft in the 1890s and to build cars from 1896-1907. The *Amilcar* was financed by *Lamy* and *Akar,* and from 1921 on developed into a very pretty little sports car, particularly the 6-cyl. 1100 cc (67 cu. in.) model with twin o.h. camshafts. The marque was absorbed by *Hotchkiss*, and *J. A. Grégoire* gave the last Amilcar front-wheel drive.

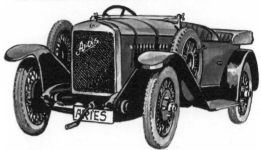

Ariès "GP2," 1928
This make was in production 1903-37, and won a high reputation in the sports-car races of the 1920s, mainly with the 3-liter (183 cu. in.) models.

Amilcar, 1925
4-cyl. 60×95 mm
$(2\frac{3}{8}'' \times 3\frac{3}{4}'')$

Ballot "2LS" engine, 1921 (69.9×130 mm, 2000 cc; $2\frac{3}{4}'' \times 5\frac{1}{8}''$, 122 cu. in.) *Ernest Henry*'s only sports-car engine followed his typical style.

Ballot "2LS"
1922

Ernest Ballot was a manufacturer of marine and automobile engines, but in 1918 he engaged Ernest Henry as a designer of racing cars; these were followed by sports cars until Hispano-Suiza took over the firm in 1931.

Bédélia, 1914. *Robert Bourbeau*'s light tandem, with passenger sandwiched between the driver and the 2-cyl. air-cooled motor, was the epitome of the cyclecar.

Berliet "22CV," 1907
4-cyl. (100 × 120 mm;
4″ × 4¾″), 3775 cc
(229 cu.in.), Landaulet

Bignan, 1922

BNC, 1929

Léon Bollée, 1924

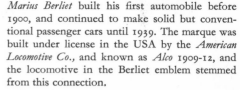

Marius Berliet built his first automobile before 1900, and continued to make solid but conventional passenger cars until 1939. The marque was built under license in the USA by the *American Locomotive Co.,* and known as *Alco* 1909-12, and the locomotive in the Berliet emblem stemmed from this connection.

Jacques Bignan made the change from producing engines to complete automobiles in 1920, and over some ten years produced several interesting cars, including a 4-cyl. 2-liter (75 × 112 mm; 3″ × 4⅜″, 122 cu.in.) car with desmodromic valves.

The firm of *Bollack, Netter & Cie* put their first automobile on the market in 1924, and the small cars which bore the factory's initials in front of their 4-cyl. *Ruby* engines were worthy examples of the small French sports car of the twenties. Production ceased during the 1930s.

The *Bollée* dynasty, of Le Mans, stretches back to the very beginnings of the industry. *Ernest-Sylvain Bollée* founded the firm in 1842; his son *Amédée* cast bells, built first-rate steam-cars, and had three sons: *Amédée* (fils), *Léon,* and *Camille.* Amédée fils and Léon each made their own cars, Léon's works being taken over by Morris in 1925.

The brothers *Angelo* and *Paul-Albert Bucciali* squandered a considerable inherited fortune during eleven years of building cars. First came the *Buc,* later the enormous *Bucciali* "TAV," which had front-wheel drive and a far-too-powerful engine (giving, in its final 16-cyl. form, some 155 bhp).

Bucciali "TAV," 1933

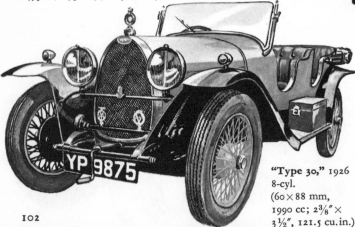

Ettore Isodoro Arco Bugatti, 1881-1947, whose life was devoted to the splendid cars from Molsheim.

"Black Bess," 1912

This chain-driven 5-liter (299 cu. in.) racing car stands at the point of transition between earlier practice and Bugatti's more advanced ideas, which were developed in the aero-engines of the war years and culminated in the 8-cyl. Type 35 engine; this made its debut in 1924 with the same dimensions as the "Type 30," and also had the earlier design's 3 valves per cylinder, but with a modified crankshaft. The stroke was increased to 100 mm (4″) in 1927.

"Type 23, Brescia," 1921

Bugatti's first model under his own name (the "Type 13") went into production at his Molsheim works in 1910. This was continued until 1924/25, together with 8-cyl. models after 1923. The "Brescia" had a 4-cyl. 16-valve engine (68 × 100 mm, 1453 cc; 2⅝″ × 4″, 88.5 cu. in.).

The **"Type 35 T"** supercharged engine (60 × 100 mm, 2270 cc; 2⅜″ × 4″, 138 cu. in.) clearly reflects Bugatti's philosophy: "Think of manufacturing when designing a part. Only round or square machining exists." Every detail component is beautifully made—although the fact that mechanical virtuosity of the highest degree was needed to assemble them into a whole was a secondary consideration. The crankshaft was in 14 parts, and ran in ball- and roller-bearings.

"Type 30," 1926
8-cyl.
(60 × 88 mm, 1990 cc; 2⅜″ × 3½″, 121.5 cu. in.)

"Type 41, La Royale," 1927/28

The two extremities of Bugatti's wide range of types are shown by the enormous "Royale" of 12,760 cc (8-cyl. 125 × 130 mm; 5″ × 5⅛″, 784 cu. in.) i/m only 7 were built, of which 6 are still in existence—and the minute "Baby," an electric scale model of the "Type 35." This was catalogued around 1930.

"Type 43," 1927—a "civilian" version of the "Type 35 T" and the cream of the classic models, with single o.h.c. and 3 valves per cylinder.

"Type 57S," 1937

"Type 55," 1931

In 1930 Bugatti, inspired by American designer *Harry Miller,* began using twin o.h. camshafts, and after working on a larger engine, incorporated the new layout in the 60 × 100 mm (2⅜″ × 4″) engine. The "type 55" sports car of 2270 cc (138 cu. in.) was developed from the "Type 51" racing model. Below is an example of his sophisticated design.

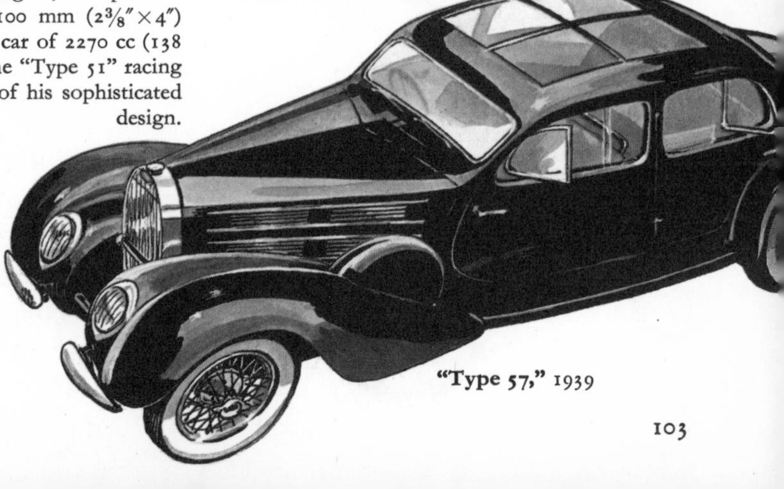

The sports version of the "Type 57" (72 × 100 mm, 3257 cc; 2⅞″ × 4″, 199 cu. in.), produced 1936-38, a supreme example of Bugatti's unique combination of road-holding with aesthetic design, carried out with superb craftsmanship. His artistic flair is evident in all his work.

"Type 57," 1939

France

Chenard & Walcker, 1927

Clément-Panhard, 1901

This firm was established in 1887, and built its first quadricycle in 1896. During the twenties it produced sturdy sports cars, whose design and styling were ahead of the times. After collaboration with *Delahaye,* front-wheel drive was tried in 1935.

Adolphe Clément was a shrewd businessman, who for a time held majority shares in Panhard-Levassor, whose chief engineer *Krebs* designed this model—a retrogression to earlier car design.

Cottin et Desgouttes, 1912

Darracq, 1904

The first car of this make appeared in 1904, and was succeeded by big, reliable cars with a sporting flavor. The crisis of 1929 forced the firm to cease production.

Alexandre Darracq was a pioneer of mass-production. His firm joined Clément-Talbot in 1919.

The *Decauville* was produced 1898-1911 by a locomotive works which saw a future in building lightweight vehicles for road use. The mechanical execution was, however, so crude that it prompted *Henry Royce,* an early customer, to build his own cars.

De Dion-Bouton, 1904

Decauville, 1898

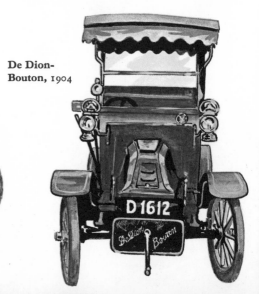

Delage "D1," 1927

Louis Delage set up as an automobile manufacturer in 1905, and made his mark with outstanding racing cars, followed by touring cars of superb quality.

During the 1920s Delage was among the leading makes technically, with first-class engines and well-designed chassis, usually coming from leading French specialists in the field. The marque consolidated its fame on the racing circuits with the formidable 2- and 1½-liter (122/91 cu.in.) models of 1923-25 and 1926-27, respectively. The former had a V-12 engine, the latter an impressive straight-8.

"D8 120," 1938

Delage went bankrupt after the 1929 slump, and was taken over in 1935 by Delahaye.

Delahaye, 1897

Emile Delahaye was a maker of brickworks machinery who foresaw possibilities in automobile manufacture. He and his able collaborators created magnificent cars, one of his leading engineers from first to last being *Charles Weiffenbach*.

Delahaye "135," 1937

"175," 1948

Delahaye won the Monte Carlo Rally several times.

Albert de Dion was, in company with *Georges Bouton*, one of the pioneers of the automotive industry. He gave his name to this back-axle design.

Using the factory's 6-cyl. truck engine, Weiffenbach built the "135" (84×107 mm, 3557 cc; 3¼"×4⅛", 217 cu.in.) which was followed by a V-12 racing car. The "135" was developed further, and in its final "235" variant of 1952 gave 158 bhp. This was the last model made before the factory amalgamated with Hotchkiss, which gave up passenger-car production a year later.

"235," 1952

De Dion axle

France

The very name *Delaunay-Belleville* did much to insure this make's success. The imposing automobiles made by the firm from 1903, with a round hood recalling their tradition of boiler manufacture, were sturdy and reliable. After 1919 the marque lost ground, although in 1946 it took over production of the *Rovin,* one of the postwar mini-cars.

Delaunay-
Belleville,
"P4B," 1926: 4-cyl. 72×120 mm, 1954 cc
(2⅞″×4¾″, 120 cu. in.)

De Dietrich, 1902

This venerable industrial firm, whose history starts well before that of the automobile, made motorcars from 1897 using designs by *Amédée Bollée* (fils), *Ettore Bugatti,* and others. The works were in Lorraine, and the emblem includes the Cross of Lorraine; for patriotic reasons the name was changed to *Lorraine-Dietrich* in 1908, and after 1919 the cars were known as *La Lorraine.* Production of cars ceased in the late 1930s, although the firm is still in business.

Ford "Vedette,"
1948

From 1934 on, the Ford assembly plant in France was managed by *Emile Mathis,* who brought out a special V-8 "Alsace" in 1935, calling it the *Matford.* In 1940 Ford Française and Mathis split up, although the "Vedette" kept the "Alsace" motor. *Simca* took over Ford's French interests in 1954.

Serpollet's steam-car was more practical than most, and the make held the world land speed record in 1902 at 75 mph.

DFP, 1914

Between 1906 and 1928 *Doriot, Flandrin et Parant* made motorcars which were very ordinary in design. *W. O. Bentley* was the British agent for the make from 1912, and carried out revolutionary experiments with aluminum pistons.

Léon Serpollet was the most ardent and inventive of the steam-car's partisans, and produced numerous designs from 1897 until his death in 1907. Production was financed by an American, *Frank Gardner.*

Gardner-Serpollet, 1904

Alexandre Darracq was a partner in the *Gladiator* cycle works, which was taken over by a British company which made motorcycles and cars from 1896, using mainly *Aster* engines. The make was quite popular in France and Britain, but was not among the more technically inspired; it faded out in 1920.

Georges Irat, 1935

This was one of the more remarkable of the many French "assembled makes." After a couple of conventional but well-built cars in the 1910s, the factory changed to front-wheel drive in 1935, using first *Ruby* and then *Citroën* engines. After 1945 came some interesting lightweight prototypes, but no series-production.

After many years' successful work on *Simca* automobiles *Amédée Gordini* became independent in 1951 and over some 5 years built various fine sports and racing cars. In the long run this proved to be an uneconomic basis for independent operation, and Gordini has since worked with Renault.

Gladiator, 1902

Tonneau body, door at rear

Gordini, 1953

6-cyl. 78 × 75 mm, 2290 cc (3⅛″ × 3″, 139 cu. in.) 150 bhp at 6000 rpm

Neither *Gustave Gobron* nor *Eugène Brillié* were prepared to follow contemporary principles in engine design, and all their cars from 1898 to 1914 used 4-cycle opposed-piston motors. These extremely complicated units were very efficient, and the make set a land speed record three times in 1903/04, the last time at 103.5 mph. *Chapuis-Dornier* engines were available from 1919.

Gobron-Brillié, 1901
2-cyl. engine with opposed pistons

J. A. Grégoire is one of the leaders of French automobile engineering, and his brilliant front-wheel drive designs have been used by several makes. He has had considerable influence on general developments by his invention of the "homokinetic" link and by fundamental scientific work. The model shown here was built by *Hotchkiss*.

Hotchkiss-Grégoire, 1950

France

Hotchkiss "AR," 1922, 6-cyl.
(100 × 140 mm; 4″ × 5½″) 6600 cc (403 cu. in.) o.h.c.

Hotchkiss "GS," 1938
6-cyl. 86 × 100 mm, 3485 cc (3⅜″ × 4″,
213 cu. in.) pushrod o.h.v.

Benjamin Berkeley Hotchkiss was an American industrialist who aided France during the Franco-Prussian War of 1870-71 by mass-production of arms. His factory's experience in precision engineering was turned to the manufacture of cars in 1903, and through various types led to the 6-cyl. engine which was used from 1934 until production ceased in 1955. The cars won the Monte Carlo Rally a number of times.

Hispano-Suiza's activity was concentrated in Paris from the early 1930s. Two imposing 6-cyl. o.h.c. models, the "H6B" and "H6C," were replaced partly by the "HS26" (a Ballot chassis with Hispano engine) and, from 1931, by the "68." This V-12 engine gave the large, heavy car a speed of over 100 mph; the marque was fitted with refined, custom-built bodies like this *Saotchik* coupé.

**Hispano-Suiza
"68-bis,"** 1934

Marc Birkigt followed Bugatti's example and made engines for railway locomotives. The "68" car engine (V-12, 100 × 100 mm, 9500 cc; 4″ × 4″, 575 cu. in.) had its stroke increased to 120 mm—4¾″ (11,300 cc—689 cu. in.) and a few cars were fitted   with this "68-bis" motor.

The Guynemer stork over the Spanish Swiss colors

André Lombard gave his name to a sports car built by BNC for *Vareille*. The racing-type engine was of 1093 cc—67 cu.in. (4-cyl. 61×92 mm; $2\frac{3}{8}'' \times 3\frac{5}{8}''$).

Lombard, 1928

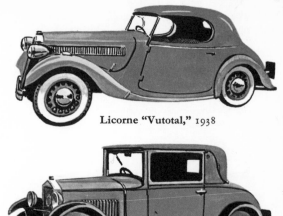

Licorne "Vutotal," 1938

Mors, 1904

Emile Mors produced some outstanding cars, and was a pioneer of the shock-absorber.

Mathis "P.Y.," 1931

Emile Mathis was a gifted designer, but his industrial interests overshadowed his technical imagination; the cars bearing his name were sound but unexceptional in design. His work for Ford of France led to the *Matford*.

Matford, 1938

During the 1920s the French automotive industry produced several inspired sports cars like the *Rally* and the *Ratier*. Very few had the financial background needed to survive the Depression, and with them died a phenomenon of great charm and some inspiration to the general technical trend. Limited production and hand assembly methods allowed frequent changes in specification and a boldness often resulting in foolhardy ventures. Nevertheless, they were great fun and very instructive to drive.

Rally, 1929

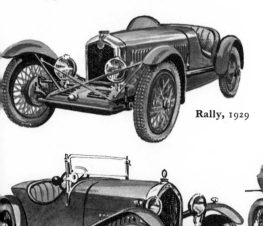

Ratier, 1927

Omega Six, 1925

France

The *Richard-Brasier* partnership (p. 99) developed their standard models from well-built cars which won the 1904 and 1905 Gordon Bennett Races and others; they found a wide sale.

Rochet-Schneider had no connection with *Th. Schneider*.

Richard-Brasier, 1905
4-cyl. (104×100 mm; 4⅛″×4″) with typical touring body.

Rochet-Schneider "26CV," 1931

A range of L-head models was followed by a valve-in-head series terminating in the "26CV."

Rosengart, 1928-29

Originally an *Austin 7* built under license, later based on an *Adler* "Trumpf," and then special versions of the *Citroën* were made under the names "Supertraction" and "Supertrahuit."

Th. Schneider,
1928

A sporting make with L-head or valve-in-head 2-liter (122 cu. in.) 4-cyl. engine. The firm produced its first car in 1910 and kept in production until the 1930s.

SARA, 1924

Société des **A***utos a* **R***efroidissement par* **A***ir* explains the name.

Salmson was taken over by Renault in 1955, and this was the last model made.

Salmson, 1924

Salmson made the change from aero-engines to cars via production of the G.N. under license. Lombard (p. 109) and *Emile Petit* financed the make, which culminated in the "San Sebastian," 1923-25.

Salmson, 1955

Sénéchal, 1921

Sima-Violet, 1926

Robert Sénéchal built ultra-light automobiles of sturdier design than most, with the backing of Chenard & Walcker.

Violet was a partisan of the 2-cycle motor, and put a 500 cc (30.5 cu.in.) air-cooled twin-cylinder engine in this light car, which was on the market 1921-27.

Sizaire-Naudin, 1909

The *Sizaire* brothers and their partner *Naudin* are remembered for automobiles of unusual designs, featuring i.f.s. and a powerful single-cyl. motor (120×140 mm; 4¾″×5″).

Sizaire-Berwick, 1921

This make (1913-25) was created by *Maurice* and *Georges Sizaire* in collaboration with the London coachbuilding firm of *F. W. Berwick*. From 1919 on it was built in London, and after 1922 disguised *Austin* cars were made.

Talbot "11/Six," 1927

The merger between *Darracq* and *Clément-Talbot* brought the British name of Talbot to France.

J.-A. Grégoire (p. 107) designed the front-wheel drive *Tracta* of 1926-30.

Tracta, 1929

Talbot "Lago-Record," 1947

Antoine Lago managed *Talbot-Darracq* after the Sunbeam-Talbot-Darracq concern was dissolved in 1935. The "Record" was developed from the racing car. The make was absorbed by Simca in 1959.

France

Turcat-Méry, 1924

This make was established before 1900, and for a time was connected with De Dietrich. T.-M. became independent after 1919, but was not strong enough to survive the Depression.

Voisin "18CV," 1920

The make's first model, with a 4-cyl. 4-liter (244 cu.in.) sleeve-valve motor (95 × 140 mm; 3¾″ × 5½″). The original engines were replaced in 1938 by *Graham* engines (p. 194).

Gabriel Voisin brought into the car business a highly original line of thought from his early days in aviation. Engines with 4, 6, 8, and 12 cylinders came from his drawing

Voisin "22CV," 1930

board, including a straight-12 in 1934. It is said that the body of the 1930 "22CV" model was inspired by Le Corbusier, but Voisin had no need for the influence of others. After 1945 he designed the "Biscuter" (p. 87).

Voisin "Aerosport," 1935

Le Zèbre "D," 1921

Jules Salomon, who designed the first 4-cyl. Le Zèbre in 1916, revised his ideas very little when creating his masterpiece, the *Citroën* "5CV" (p. 88).

Nicolas Joseph Cugnot's steam tractor is quite overwhelming by its sheer size. The impression is heightened by the patina on the heavy wooden beams and by the impressive dimensions of the metal parts. But the vehicle is not merely large—it is magnificent in its conception, and bears witness to the fertile imagination of its creator. Today it is easy to point out the weaknesses of the design— the whole of the heavy power unit turns with the front wheel as it steers, the boiler is of limited capacity and cannot be refilled under way (giving only 10-12 minutes running time), and the vehicle can only be brought to a halt by letting the steam escape. Similar criticisms of poor steering, an indadequate fuel reserve, and indadequate brakes can, however, be leveled at several modern cars, despite all the theoretical and practical experience amassed since 1769 when Cugnot built his fiirst model.

The best features of Cugnot's design are the twin-cylinder single-acting steam engine, in which the steam pressure is automatically distributed to the two pistons, and its incorporation in a vehicle, plus the sophisticated solution he found to the mechanical problems of transmission. Cugnot was so far ahead of the technical possibilities of his time that the result inevitably had only limited practical significance. The Cugnot tractor forms a prized example of the pioneering achievements of French engineering, and one of the highlights of my motoring experiences was to be able—thanks to the extraordinary kindness of the *Conservatoire National des Arts et Métiers*—to sit in the driving seat. Perched a full six feet above the ground, with a view out over the massive steering handle, the lever for the stop-valve, the two cylinders, and the round, copper boiler, it was possible to share the dreams of the very first motorist.

Cugnot, 1771

Twin-cyl. (325×305 mm; 12⅞″×12″) single-acting steam engine, automatic pressure feed between the cylinders through rotating valves; wood fire under the boiler. Wooden chassis, without springs; total length 285″, wheelbase 121″, tread 69″, total width 87″; height 87″, wheel diameter 50½″ front, 79″ rear; front-wheel drive (pawl mechanism from connecting rods), rack-and-pinion steering; load capacity 4-5 tons, max. speed about 2½ mph.

British cars are a mixed bag. Many contradictory tendencies have influenced—and continue to influence—the industry's organization, conditions, and aims, with the result that both makes and models have been extremely numerous. A blend of insular prejudice, commercially unpromising experience with steam buses 1820-40, and a mistaken keenness to protect obsolete interests gave the industry a hesitant start. Before, and more particularly after, the change in legislation of 1896 which made it practicable to drive an automobile, *Harry John Lawson* was engaged in elaborate financial maneuvers which came close to ruining the infant industry, which he was intent on welding into a single, powerful combine. All this did not, however, deter some individual eccentrics from building or importing their own cars, and it was from this private enthusiasm that British automobile manufacture grew. The later,

serious industry had to take into account this personal tradition, which is still very strong; there can be no other explanation for the mass-production of identical cars with different badges on the radiator, and the like. Consideration for distributors and dealers is hardly the determining factor. Up to 1931 every British automobile factory jealously guarded the "image" of its own make; then followed ten years of stagnating tradition and widespread mediocrity, but fierce competition in the export markets after 1945 brought about both a concentration of production and a refreshingly new technical outlook. Despite far-reaching standardization there is still a place for individual ideas, and British factories produce a more varied selection of vehicles than those of other countries. Some makes have been able to maintain their traditions from the days of the carriage trade, and others from the sporting period of the 1920s. However, a fresh approach by designers has made possible something that the industry itself had been unable to achieve—the building of Grand Prix racing cars which have completely changed previous conceptions of what was feasible in automobile engineering. Annual production in Britain is over 1,300,000.

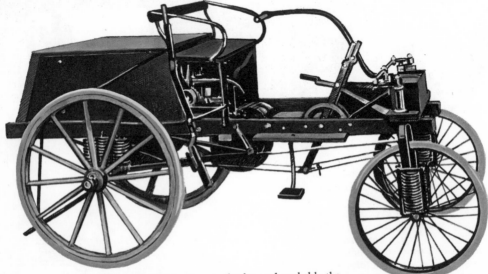

Knight, 1895. Originally a 3-wheeler, and probably the earliest British gasoline-engined vehicle to run on a public highway.

AC "Sociable,"
1907

AC "Royal," 1926

The *Auto-Carrier* company built light 3-wheeled commercial vehicles from 1904, and also made the "Sociable" which was halfway between a car and a motorcycle. The first 4-wheeler came in 1918, and in 1919 the company introduced *John Weller*'s outstanding 6-cyl. 2-liter engine (65 × 100 mm [122 cu.in., 2⅝" × 4"] single o.h.c., light alloy construction, orig. 40 bhp, now 103 bhp) which it has used ever since. Nowadays, Bristol and modified Ford "Zephyr" engines are also available. AC won the Monte Carlo Rally in 1926.

AC "2-liter," 1947

AC "Aceca," 1955

From 1954 onward AC went over to independent suspension on all four wheels, and at the same time adopted modern bodywork without losing their individuality of style.

Allard Special,
1938

Sydney Allard modified a Ford V-8 for "mud-plugging" trials, and took up limited production of sports cars.

Allard "P1," 1952

After 1945 Allards had British and American proprietary engines, and won the Monte Carlo Rally in 1952. Now they only supply conversions for series-production cars.

Allard "J2," 1951

"12/50," 1925/26

The name *Alvis* was made up by the designer *G.P.H. de Freville,* who together with *T. G. John* planned the first model in 1918. The L-head "10/30" was replaced in 1923 by the valve-in-head "12/50," a very pleasant car designed by *G. T. Smith-Clarke.* A highly interesting front-wheel-drive racing car followed two years later, with a chassis design later used for sports cars ("12/75"). The Depression brought about a change in production policy, and various rear-wheel-drive models culminated in 1937 in the 6-cyl. 4.3-liter (244 cu.in.) model (92 × 100 mm; $3\frac{5}{8}'' \times 4''$) which had 9 small coil springs surrounding each valve stem—five wound right-handed and four left-handed: a typical, painstaking design detail.

"12/75 Alvista," 1929

After a less-inspired postwar 4-cyl. model came a promising 3-liter (183 cu.in.) car in 1950. This led to collaboration with the Swiss coach-building firm of *Hermann Graber* and the development of the TD model, with bodywork built in England under license. Designs by *Alec Issigonis* for a V-8 engine in a new chassis were dropped in 1955.

TD "21," 1962

Lionel Martin called his first car the *Aston Martin,* after the Aston Clinton hill climb, and together with *R. Bamford* he produced a s.v. *Bamford & Martin Aston* from 1922. The firm was taken over in 1926 by *W. S. Renwick* and *A. C. Bertelli,* and achieved outstanding sporting successes. Since 1947 the make has belonged to the *David Brown* concern, and has used *W. O. Bentley*'s postwar *Lagonda* engine.

Bamford & Martin Aston, 1924

The Le Mans model of 1933 (*below*) was typical of the marque's superb 1½-liter (91½ cu.in.) models.

"DB4 GT," 1960

The DB models were partly intended for sports-car racing and partly for fast touring. The original engine has been revised, and it is now a highly developed, expensive car for the connoisseur.

Austin "25/30 HP," 1906

Herbert Austin (1866-1941) started with *Wolseley,* who made sheep-shearing machinery but built automobiles from 1895.

"Twelve," 1921   "Seven," 1926

It is said that only one of Austin's 3-wheeler 1895 models for *Wolseley* was made; but he went on to produce a million or more cars. The Austin "Seven" was the first small 4-cyl. automobile to go into really large-scale production. The model's name was retained until 1962 in spite of the make's merger with the Nuffield concern to form the *British Motor Corporation.*

Austin-Healey "100," 1955

"A99 Westminster," 1961

Production of *Donald Healey's* sports car with an Austin engine was begun in 1952, the year after Nuffield and Austin had formed BMC.

Austin-Healey "Sprite," 1958

117

"3-liter Vanden Plas," 1924
4-cyl. 80×149 mm ($3\frac{1}{8}'' \times 5\frac{7}{8}''$)

Walter Owen Bentley considers the *Bentley BR2* rotary aeromotor of 1918 to be his greatest technical triumph. This was succeeded in 1919 by his first car, planned in 1914. The 4-cyl. "3-liter" was in series-production 1921–29. The 6-cyl. "$6\frac{1}{2}$ liter" appeared in 1925, and was supplemented in 1931 by the sumptuous "8-liter."

"$4\frac{1}{2}$-liter Supercharged," 1930

YU 3250

The 4-cyl. 4398 cc—269 cu.in. (100×140 mm; $4'' \times 5\frac{1}{2}''$) Bentley of 1928-31 was fitted with a supercharger by *Sir Henry Birkin*. The factory itself built 50 cars of this type which, although not Bentley's own favorite, gave Birkin an unforgettable second place in the 1930 French Grand Prix.

"8-liter" 6-cyl. 110×140 mm ($4\frac{3}{8}'' \times 5\frac{1}{2}''$)

Bentley built large and strong. The cars evoked his apprentice years with the *Great Northern Railway,* and demonstrate his uncompromising mechanical philosophy. The successes of his large cars are legendary, and five Le Mans victories plus innumerable records make this one of the most respected makes.

"Speed-Six," 1929/30

AC 260

The Bentley radiator badge was designed by *F. Gordon-Crosby,* the famous illustrator of *The Autocar,* and various colors have been used—to some extent as a means of distinguishing the different types and models (Red Label, Blue Label, etc.). As the factory was forced to close down during the Depression, the name, the make, and Bentley himself were taken over by Rolls-Royce, although the cars from *Bentley Motors* (1931) *Ltd.* have nothing to do with the design work of W. O. Bentley.

Bentley "3½-liter," 1933

After some vacillation, Rolls-Royce fitted a "20/25" engine in a new chassis and with a Bentley radiator shell to produce "The Silent Sports Car"; it was more "silent" than "sports."

Bentley "4¼-liter," 1939

The new Bentley, whose 6-cyl. motor (82×114 mm; 3¼″×4½″) had all the Rolls-Royce qualities, also had excellent brakes although it lacked the necessary horsepower. The engine size was accordingly increased to 4¼ liters (89×114 mm; 260 cu.in., 3½″×4½″) from 1937 onward, and this model was capable of around 95 mph. With overdrive it was a slightly faster and more attractive car, although the old "bite" was missing. After 1945 the technical similarity with Rolls-Royce became even more pronounced, and the make's significance as a status symbol was carefully nurtured. The sporting flavor, which had still been present in 1939, disappeared completely, although the "Continental" introduced, at first for export only, in 1951 did make some concession to the character of the original marque with a very impressive performance. The Rolls-Royce V-8 engine (104.4×91.4 mm, 6230 cc; 4⅛″×3⅝″, 380 cu.in.) is also used in the Bentley "S2" series. Only the radiator shell serves to distinguish the two makes—apart from the price (the Bentley is $300 or so cheaper).

Bentley "S2"

Bentley "Continental," 1958

Great Britain

The Berkeley was an offshoot of the trailer firm of the same name. The front-wheel drive car began with a 2-cycle engine, and later had a 4-cycle unit. A rear-wheel-drive model was brought out in 1960, but production ceased soon after.

Berkeley "B95"
1959

Bristol "400," 1947

Bristol aircraft factory allied itself with *Frazer-Nash,* which sold BMW cars in Britain, and in 1945 established *Bristol Cars Ltd.*; the automobiles used a revised BMW "328" engine.

Bristol kept the BMW-inspired motor until late 1961; as it was then impossible to enlarge or develop it further, the factory went over to using a Canadian Chrysler V-8 (98.6 × 84 mm, 5130 cc; $3\frac{7}{8}'' \times 3\frac{1}{4}''$, 313 cu.in.) and at the same time made certain modifications to the chassis. This model, the "407," is identical with the "406" in appearance.

Bristol "406," 1960

John Cooper and his father *Charles* started "manufacturing" with a 500 cc (30.5 cu.in.) racing car in 1946. After dominating the Formula 3 scene with the later developments of this, Cooper tried making front-engined sports cars, but went back to their original rear-engine layout when the 1100 cc (67 cu.in.) *Coventry-Climax* engine became available in 1955.

This sports car was intended purely for racing, and it was, indirectly, of great importance as being the real forerunner of the Formula 2 car, which in turn became the Formula 1 Cooper that gave *Jack Brabham* the World Driver's Championship in 1959 and 1960 and at the same time ended the earlier dominance of Italian makes.

Cooper, 1955

1897: 2-cyl.
90 × 120 mm
1527 cc
(3⅝″ × 4¾″,
93.5 cu.in.)

The *Daimler Motor Syndicate* was founded in 1893 to acquire the British rights, held by Frederick R. Simms, of *Gottlieb Daimler*'s engine patents. The company changed to the *Daimler Motor Co. Ltd.* in 1896, and formed part of the grandiose schemes of *H. J. Lawson*. When these failed the company was re-formed, and in 1910 became part of the *Birmingham Small Arms* concern. The first car was built in 1897; sleeve-valve motors were used 1909-35; "fluid flywheel" and preselector gearbox 1931-57. The factory was absorbed by *Jaguar* in 1960.

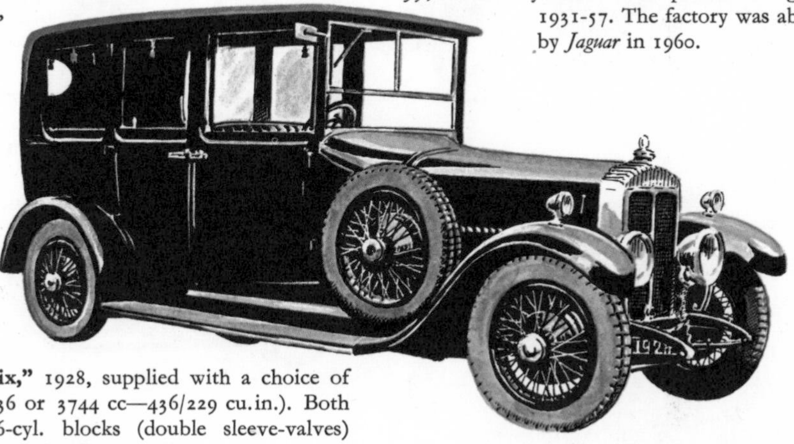

"Double Six," 1928, supplied with a choice of motors (7136 or 3744 cc—436/229 cu.in.). Both had two 6-cyl. blocks (double sleeve-valves) behind the fluted radiator shell.

"Straight Eight"
1948

"SP 250," 1961
V-8, 76.2 × 69.9 mm,
2549 cc
(3″ × 2¾″, 155.4 cu.in.).

Frank Nichols built his first Elva in 1955. Limited series-production from 1958; manufactured by *Trojan Ltd* since 1962 (p. 145).

Elva

Donald Bennett brought out his Fairthorpe "Atom" economy car in 1954, and followed this with lightweight sports cars.

Fairthorpe

"Courier," 1958

"Zeta," 1961

Great Britain

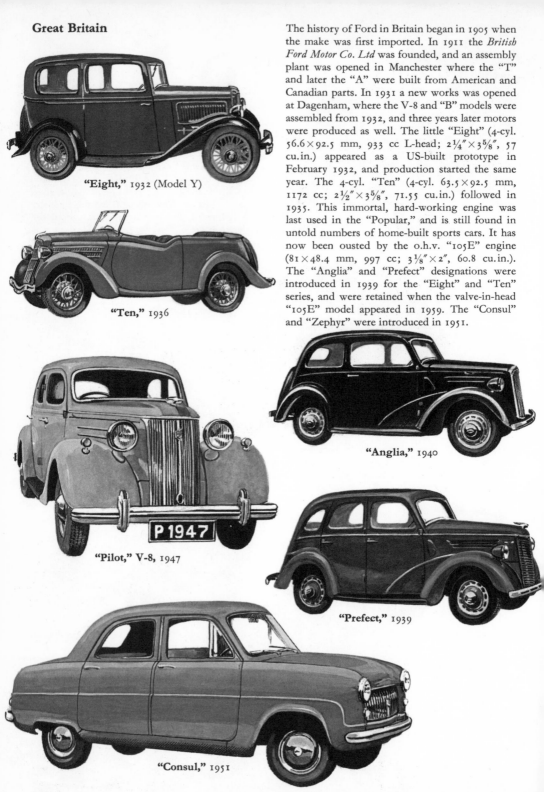

The history of Ford in Britain began in 1905 when the make was first imported. In 1911 the *British Ford Motor Co. Ltd* was founded, and an assembly plant was opened in Manchester where the "T" and later the "A" were built from American and Canadian parts. In 1931 a new works was opened at Dagenham, where the V-8 and "B" models were assembled from 1932, and three years later motors were produced as well. The little "Eight" (4-cyl. 56.6×92.5 mm, 933 cc L-head; 2¼"×3⅝", 57 cu.in.) appeared as a US-built prototype in February 1932, and production started the same year. The 4-cyl. "Ten" (4-cyl. 63.5×92.5 mm, 1172 cc; 2½"×3⅝", 71.55 cu.in.) followed in 1935. This immortal, hard-working engine was last used in the "Popular," and is still found in untold numbers of home-built sports cars. It has now been ousted by the o.h.v. "105E" engine (81×48.4 mm, 997 cc; 3⅛"×2", 60.8 cu.in.). The "Anglia" and "Prefect" designations were introduced in 1939 for the "Eight" and "Ten" series, and were retained when the valve-in-head "105E" model appeared in 1959. The "Consul" and "Zephyr" were introduced in 1951.

"Eight," 1932 (Model Y)

"Ten," 1936

"Pilot," V-8, 1947

"Anglia," 1940

"Prefect," 1939

"Consul," 1951

The "Consul" and "Zephyr" series of 1951 were a technical watershed for British Ford, then adopting an integral body-frame construction, i.f.s. and valve-in-head motors of 4 and 6 cylinders respectively (79.4 × 76.2 mm, 1508 and 2262 cc; $3\frac{1}{8}'' \times 3''$, 92/138 cu.in.). The body styling was altered in 1956, and the "Zodiac" de luxe version of the Zephyr was introduced in 1954. The series was revised in 1962, becoming the "Mk III Zephyr 4" and "6."

Great Britain

"Zodiac," 1957

"Anglia 105 E," 1960

This model was a clear breakaway from British Ford traditions, introducing a 4-speed transmission and a very high-revving, over-square motor.

The rear window was inspired by earlier experiments by Italian custom coach-builders.

The "Consul Classic 315" follows the pattern of the "105E Anglia" both in mechanical features and outward appearance. This model appeared in 1961. In price and size it comes between the "Zephyr 4" (ex-"Consul") and the "Consul Cortina" introduced in 1962.

"Consul Classic 315," 1961
4-cyl. 81 × 65.1 mm, 1340 cc
($3\frac{1}{8}'' \times 2\frac{5}{8}''$, 81 cu.in.)

Archie Frazer-Nash carried on the traditions of the *G. N.* (p. 142), and from 1924 onward built the famous "Chaingang" sports cars, with various engines and chain-drive without a differential.

"Ulster 100," 1937

"Le Mans," 1950

A light but strong chassis, rigid axles on quarter-elliptic springs, chain-drive and gearshift with dog clutches plus a powerful engine was the recipe for the classic Frazer-Nash. The *Aldington* brothers took over the make and after 1934 they concentrated on the import of BMWs. Since 1945 the marque has been a highly specialized development of the BMW (see Bristol, p. 120).

Hillman-Coatalen "12/15"
1908 (4-cyl. 89×95 mm, 2300 cc; 3½"×3¾", 144.3 cu.in.) Followed by two models with larger 4- and 6-cyl. engines.

Hillman "Minx," 1931
4-cyl. 63×95 mm, 1185 cc
(2½"×3¾", 72 cu.in.)

Over the years Hillman had produced many different models of various sizes, none of them particularly noteworthy. In 1928 the firm came under the management of *William* and *Reginald Rootes*.

In 1907 *William Hil man* joined forces with the designer *Louis Coatalen,* who came from *Humber* and quickly moved on to *Sunbeam* after marrying Miss Hillman. This French designer played an important role in the British automobile industry.

Hillman "10HP," 1921 (4-cyl. 63×120 mm, 1496 cc; 2½"×4¾", 91.5 cu.in.) was a sturdy car, foreshadowing the later "Minx" models.

"Aero Minx," 1933 (4-cyl. 63×95 mm, 1185 cc; 2½"×3¾", 72 cu.in.), a sports version of the "Minx," took the place of the "Husky" sports car which had appeared in 1928.

The "Minx," which appeared in prototype form in 1931, was a successful family car with no sporting pretensions at all. Rootes have kept pace with changing technical needs, and developed the model into the latest "Super Minx."

"Minx Mk VIII," 1955 (4-cyl. 76.2×76.2 mm, 1390 cc; 3"×3", 84.8 cu.in.), first o.h.v. model. The motor was developed for the *Sunbeam* "Rapier" of 1956.

"Minx IIIa," 1961 (4-cyl. 79×76.2 mm, 1494 cc 3⅛"×3", 91.5 cu.in.)

Humber "Sociable," 1898

"Humberette," 1904

Thomas Humber's velocipede and cycle works was founded in 1867, and entered the car industry through the financial ventures of H. J. Lawson as a licensed producer of *Léon Bollée* tricycles. Humber had previously produced prototypes of the *Pennington* and other curious vehicles in harmony with Lawson's highly colored schemes. The "Sociable" was a modified Bollée with an engine designed by *C. McRobie Turrell.*

Around the turn of the century Humber was reformed outside Lawson's tottering empire, and a successful light car with the single-cylinder *De Dion* motor was added to the earlier models. This "Humberette" series was continued, with improvements, for a number of years. The cars were built in both Coventry and Beeston, although gradually production of the larger models was concentrated at Beeston. The works were brought together at Coventry during 1908-1909, and the company was again reorganized. In 1928 Humber joined forces with *Hillman* as part of the *Rootes* concern.

Humber "14/40,"
1928

After the early, stormy years Humber found a sober style, reflected in all its products 1918-32. Without possessing any remarkable technical features—apart from an F-head motor 1922-32—Humber was known for honest quality and a certain robust charm.

"Old Faithful"

Field-Marshal *Lord Montgomery*'s staff car during the Mediterranean campaign 1942-43 was a 6-cyl. (85 × 120 mm, 4086 cc; 3¼″ × 4¾″, 249 cu. in.) 1941 Humber "Super Snipe."

The **"Vogue 12hp"** of 1934 had very daring lines for that period. It was styled by Capt. Molyneux, London dress designer.

"Super Snipe," 1962

Austin "Seven," 1931, with body by the *Swallow Sidecar & Coachbuilding Co.,* the predecessor of *Jaguar.*

"SS I, 20 hp Tourer," 1933

(6-cyl. 73 × 101.6 mm, 2552 cc; 2⅞″ × 4″, 155.8 cu.in.)

"SS I, 16 hp," 1934/35 (6-cyl. 65.5 × 106 mm, 2143 cc [2⅝″ × 4¼″, 130 cu.in.]; 20 hp: 73 × 106 mm, 2664 cc [2⅞″ × 4¼″, 163 cu.in.]) was an astute development of the bizarre but successful lines of the first SS coupé of 1932.

SS "Airline," 1935

SS "100" 1938 (6 cyl. 73 × 106 mm, 2664 cc; 2⅞″ × 4⅛″, 162.4 cu.in.). SS introduced their first sports car, the "90", in 1935, and next year the "100".

The transformation from *William Lyons'* first *Swallow* sidecar, made in 1922 in company with *William Walmsley,* to the *Jaguar* and the superb XK engines, is one of the fairy tales of the automobile industry. From modest beginnings in Blackpool, he progressed after 1927 to making custom bodies (for Austin, Morris, Fiat, Standard, Swift, and Wolseley) and grew into the *Swallow Sidecar & Coachbuilding Co.* which moved to Coventry in 1928. Three years later the *SS* car appeared; the letters have been translated as "Standard Swallow" or "Swallow Sports," but they are not in fact an abbreviation. The make was based on a specially built *Standard* chassis, with sporting body lines, but had a quite modest performance. The quality of trim was, however, out of all proportion to the price. In 1936 the first SS Jaguar model was introduced; in 1945 the meaningless and perhaps slightly sinister initials were dropped. With the XK engines on which chief engineer *W. M. Heynes* had been working during the war years, *Jaguar Cars Ltd.* occupied a new place in the world market after 1948. To lavish trim was added tremendous performance, active racing experience, and numerous victories (including Le Mans in 1951, '53, '55, '56, and '57), countless honors, rising production, and the acquisition of the *Daimler, Guy,* and *Coventry-Climax* companies.

SS "Jaguar, 3½ liter," 1939 (6-cyl. 82 × 110 mm, 3485 cc; 3¼″ × 4⅜″, 212 cu.in.)

"Mk V," 1949-51 transitional model, last to have the pushrod motor.

SIR WILLIAM LYONS

"XK120," 1949-54

"MK VII," 1951-57

JAGUAR CARS LTD. · COVENTRY

"3.8-liter Mk 2," 1961

"E-Type," 1961

The 6-cyl. **XK** engines are the result of extensive experiments 1945-48, and follow classic sports racing lines with two overhead camshafts. The original engine size (83 × 106 mm, 3442 cc; $3\frac{1}{4}$" × $4\frac{1}{8}$", 210 cu.in.) has been supplemented by the 2.4 and 3.8-liter types.

The **"XK 120 C"** (1951-54) was a sports car for serious racing. It was replaced by the **"D-Type"** (1955-57). Disc brakes were adopted in 1953, after exhaustive testing. From this car were developed the **"E-Type"** and the **"Mk X"** of 1962.

"Mk X," 1962

127

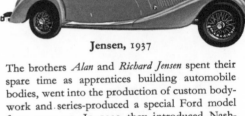

Jensen-Ford, 1934

Jensen, 1937

Jensen "541 S," 1961

The brothers *Alan* and *Richard Jensen* spent their spare time as apprentices building automobile bodies, went into the production of custom body-work and series-produced a special Ford model from 1934 on. In 1939 they introduced Nash-engined models with most attractive body lines. The "541" with fiberglass bodywork and an Austin engine was introduced for 1954 and built in limited numbers. The "C-V8," with a 5.9-liter Chrysler motor, was introduced at the 1962 London Motor Show.

Lagonda "11.1 hp," 1913

Wilbur Gunn came to England from the USA, worked with steamships, and from 1898 built motorcycles, tricars, and automobiles named *Lagonda* after a tributary of the Mad River. The "V-12" was a highlight among many good models.

The story goes that *Colin Chapman* called his first trials car *Lotus* after his sweetheart, later to become his wife; her name, however, was Hazel. Right from his first Austin-based car, built in 1947/48, Chapman had a bold and unconventional approach. He applied his ultra-lightweight building methods to sports cars, the later "Elite," "Elan," and pure GP cars.

Lotus "Seven," 1960

Offering no concessions to comfort, but outstanding road-holding, the "Seven" is also available in kit form (tuned Ford engine).

Lagonda "V-12," 1938

"Elite," 1958

"2½-liter," 1947

W. O. Bentley created the "V-12" and "2½-liter." The David Brown company took over in 1947.

The suspension results from unique racing experience and the monocoque fiberglass body was a daring innovation. A *Coventry-Climax* motor (4-cyl. 76.2×66.6 mm, 1216 cc; 3″× 2⅝″, 74.25 cu.in.) gives speeds over 112 mph.

"MG Kimber Special," 1925

"M-type Midget," 1929
4-cyl. 57 × 83 mm, 847 cc (2¼″ × 3¼″, 51.5 cu.in.)

MG **"Mk III,"** 1930
6-cyl.(69 × 110 mm, 2468 cc; 2¾″ × 4⅜″, 150 cu.in.)

As manager of *Morris Garages*—the firm from which Morris Motors had evolved and which remains their Oxford sales outlet—*Cecil Kimber* amused himself by giving the contemporary "Oxford" a more sporting performance. The result caught on, and a new make was born, using the initials of its birthplace. The first, rather tame series was followed by more sporting cars — the Mk IV (4-cyl. 1800 cc — 109 cu.in.) and Mk I, II, and III (6-cyl. 2500 cc—150 cu.in.)—in that order.

"K3 Magnette," 1934
6-cyl. (57 × 71 mm, 1087 cc; 2¼″ × 2¾″, 66.5 cu.in.) supercharged. The standardization which followed the *Nuffield* merger in BMC affected MG as well, and the latest "Midget" is a disguised Austin-Healey.

Model **"WA,"** 1939, 6-cyl. (73 × 102 mm, 2561 cc; 2⅞″ × 4″, 156 cu.in.). The "Magna" and "Magnette" models appeared 1932-36, and the "SA," "VA," and "WA" 1936-39.

The first 6-cyl. Mks I and II were superseded in 1933 by the popular "Midget" series, which began in 1929 with the "M-type" (a modified *Morris* "Minor.")

MG **"TC,"** 1946

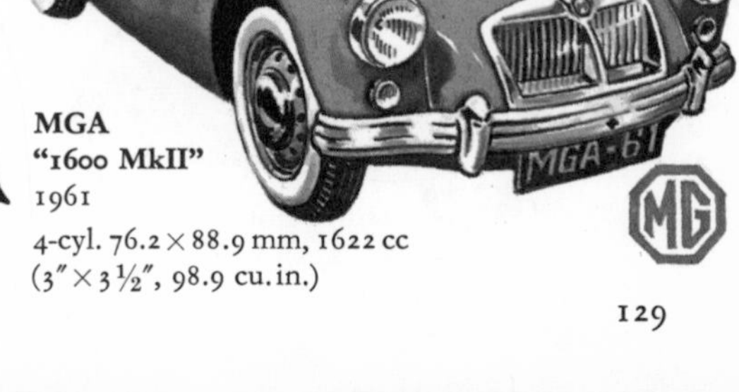

MGA
"1600 MkII"
1961
4-cyl. 76.2 × 88.9 mm, 1622 cc (3″ × 3½″, 98.9 cu.in.)

MG

Morgan "J. A. P. Super Sports"
1931, 2-cyl. air-cooled motorcycle motor

H. F. S. Morgan was a refreshing individualist. The same i.f.s. system has been used from the first 3-wheeler in 1909 to the present day. The 3-wheeled "Moggie" was joined in 1936 by a full-size car, the Morgan 4/4, and the last "threeler" was delivered in 1951. Various motors have been used; the "Plus 4" has a "TR3" unit, and the "Series II 4/4" the 105E from the *Ford* "Anglia."

Morgan "Plus Four"
1958

William Richard Morris, later *Lord Nuffield,* began his incredible career as a bicycle mechanic, progressed to being a motorcycle manufacturer and garage owner (Morris Garages), and started making cars in 1912. His robust productions laid the foundations of the Nuffield empire, which apart from its *MG* offshoot absorbed *Wolseley* (1927) and *Riley* (1938) as well as a number of component suppliers. Since 1951 the Nuffield group has been in partnership with *Austin* in the *British Motor Corporation,* where a far-reaching policy of technical rationalization has been applied.

"Minor," 1929

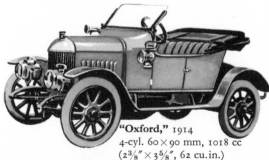

"Oxford," 1914
4-cyl. 60×90 mm, 1018 cc
(2⅜″×3⅝″, 62 cu.in.)

Despite its o.h. camshaft the first "Minor" was an economy car. The brilliant 1948 design of *Alec Issigonis* also aimed at economy, combined with outstanding road-holding. His front-wheel drive "Mini-Minor" and "1100" with their transverse engines are delightfully unorthodox.

"Minor," 1948

"Mini-Minor," 1959
alias Austin **"Seven"**

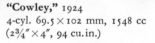

"Cowley," 1924
4-cyl. 69.5×102 mm, 1548 cc
(2¾″×4″, 94 cu.in.)

Morris
"Oxford," 1956   **"Oxford,"** 1961

Austin "Princess IV," 1957;
a separate make after 1958

Princess "3-liter," 1961

Riley

Riley "9hp," 1907
2-cyl. 86×89 mm, 1034 cc
(3⅜″×3½″, 62.6 cu. in.)

"Brooklands Nine," 1928

From 1898 until 1956 the marque founded by
William Riley retained its individual specification,
although it is now a standardized BMC product.

"Imp," 1935; 4-cyl.
63.3×95.2 mm, 1089 cc
(2½″×3¾″, 66.5 cu. in.)

"1½-liter," 1946-55
69×100 mm, 1496 cc
(2¾″×4″, 91.5 cu. in.)

"Adelphi," 1938

4-cyl. 69×100 mm
1496 cc (2¾″×4″, 91.5 cu. in.)

"One-Point-Five," 1961 — a modified Wolseley

CHARLES STUART ROLLS
1877-1910

FREDERICK HENRY ROYCE
1863-1933

Rolls-Royce "10hp," 1905
twin-cylinder

"Legalimit" 1905, V-8 engine, 83 × 83 mm (3¼"
× 3¼"); designed as a town carriage, to compete
with the electric broughams.

F. H. Royce began in very humble circumstances,
and through great ability and constant hard work
built up a thriving electrical engineering business.
In 1903 he bought a *Decauville,* but considered it
such an inferior piece of engineering that in
desperation he decided to build a properly made
car himself. This very first *Royce* was so faultless
that the Hon. *C. S. Rolls* took on the marketing
of it under the name of *Rolls-Royce*. As an engineer
Royce strove relentlessly for mechanical perfection; Rolls was a dashing pioneer of motor sport
and flying. Their widely differing temperaments
were held together by the skillful
organization of *Claude Johnson.*

"Silver Ghost," 1906

"London-Edinburgh"
1911

"Phantom I," 1925, 6-cyl. 108 × 139 mm, 7668 cc
(4¼″ × 5½″, 468 cu. in.)

"Twenty," 1928
6-cyl. 76.2 × 114.3 mm,
3200 cc (3″ × 4½″, 190.8 cu. in.)

"Phantom II," 1933
modernized "P I"

Rolls-Royce showed the "40/50" model (p. 132) at the 1906 London Motor Show. Known as the "Silver Ghost," it was in production until 1926. The 6-cyl. began as 114 × 114 mm (4½″ × 4½″) and ended as 114 × 121 mm (4½″ × 4¾″), 7400 cc (453 cu. in.) in 1926. Its successor, the "Phantom I," was produced 1925-29, and was followed by the "Phantom II" 1929-36. The "Twenty" was a "small" R. R., introduced in 1922 and later supplied with a bigger motor. The marque's uncontested slogan "The Best Car in the World" reflects no boldly original mechanical features, but rather an unsurpassed attention to detail and an inexorable insistence on quality. The same characteristics are found in the firm's aero-engines, and cars have come to form only a small proportion of R.R. output. The 6-cyl. "Silver Wraith" models produced from 1946, and the "Phantom IV" introduced in 1950 with an 8-in-line motor, were both replaced in 1959 by the V-8 "Silver Cloud II" series (104.1 × 91.7 mm, 6230 cc; 4⅛″ × 3⅝″, 380 cu. in.), the longest chassis being known as the "Phantom V."

"Phantom III," 1938

This car (V-12, 82.5 × 114.3 mm, 7340 cc; 3¼″ × 4½″, 448 cu. in.) of 1936-38 was the first R.R. to have i.f.s., and the last of the Classic models.

"Silver Cloud II," 1962

"20hp," 1907, 4-cyl. 97 × 110 mm, 3256 cc (3¾″ × 4⅜″, 198.5 cu.in.)—the lighest car in its class, and winner of the 1907 *Tourist Trophy*.

"Twelve," 1912
4-cyl. 75 × 130 mm
2300 cc (3″ × 5⅛″, 140 cu.in.)

"8hp" chassis, 1904
1-cyl. 114 × 130 mm
1250 cc (4½″ × 5⅛″,
76.3 cu.in.)

The bicycle pioneer *J. K. Starley* was one of the founders of *The Rover Cycle Co.* in 1896. Motorcycles quickly appeared, and were followed in 1904 by unconventional cars with a cast-aluminum backbone chassis. This model, designed by *E. W. Lewis,* enjoyed great popularity. The make's bigger models, too, were well-built cars, and the smaller "Twelve" which replaced the single-cylinder model in 1912 was of high technical quality. It was designed by *Owen Clegg.* The factory has kept its well-merited position through the years, and is further consolidating its fame with interesting experimental gas-turbine automobiles.

"Twelve Sports Tourer," 1934
4-cyl. 69 × 100 mm,
1496 cc (2¾″ × 4″, 91.5 cu.in.)

Rover **"Jet 1,"** the world's first turbine car, was demonstrated on March 8, 1950, and was succeeded by several successful experimental cars.

"100," 1961, 6-cyl. 77.8 × 92.1 mm, 2625 cc (3⅛″ × 3⅝″, 160 cu.in.)

The *Coventry Sewing Machine Company* took on a bicycle contract in 1868, and among the engineers employed on this was *George Singer*. He opened his own cycle-building business in 1876, and in 1900 added motor-cycles. He built his first car in 1904, and began regular series-production in 1905.

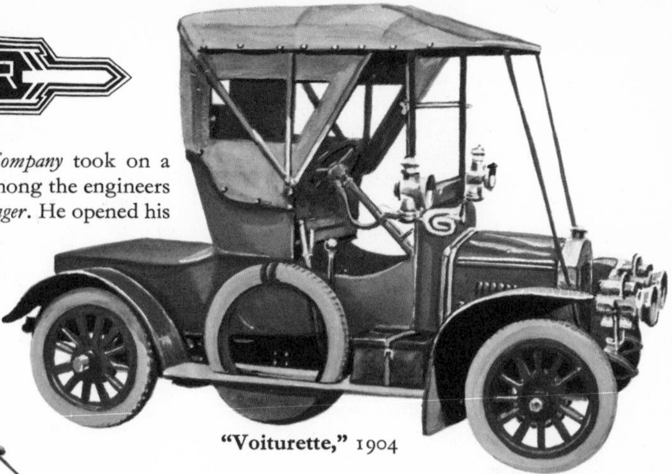

"Voiturette," 1904

When the Singer "Ten" was launched, a car dealer named *William Rootes* took the whole year's output. During the 1930s the marque made its name in motor sport, and the 4-cyl. engines—of varying sizes but all o.h.c.—were continued in the "SM" and "Hunter" series. In 1956 the Rootes Group took over the make, which became a crossbreed of *Hillman* and *Sunbeam*.

"Ten," 1912

4-cyl. 63×88 mm, 1097 cc (2½″×3½″, 67 cu.in.). This model, with gearbox mounted on the differential in the back axle, brought renown through sporting wins.

"Le Mans Nine," 1935
4-cyl. 60×86 mm, 972 cc (2⅜″×3⅜″, 59 cu.in.)

"SM 1500, Roadster," 1951
4-cyl. 73×89.4 mm, 1497 cc (2⅞″×3½″, 91.5 cu.in.)

"Hunter," 1955

After the Rootes take-over, the Singer motor was kept for a short while, but was then replaced by a slightly modified Hillman unit. The same body is also shared, with a few detail changes. The "Vogue" corresponds to the Hillman "Super Minx."

"Vogue," 1962

Great Britain

The Standard Motor Car Company was founded in 1903 by *R. W. Maudslay,* who planned to produce a limited number of models with standardized, interchangeable parts. This policy is implicit in the name. The original principles were soon dropped, and many different models appeared until the Depression made a drastic overhaul of the firm necessary. This was carried out by *John Black,* who introduced the "Flying Standard" models in 1935. They reflected the factory's 1914-18 production of military planes, and foreshadowed the 1939-45 output of aero-engines and Mosquito aircraft.

Triumph was acquired in 1945, and the *Ferguson* tractor was built under license. *Standard-Triumph International* later got into difficulties, and was bought out by *Leyland Motors Ltd.* in 1961.

"6hp," 1903 **"standard-model"**
1-cyl. 127×76.2 mm, 1390 cc
(5″×3″, 84.8 cu.in.)

"11.4hp," 1920, 68×110 mm, 1597 cc (2⅝″×4⅜″, 97 cu.in.)

"24/30 hp," 1906, 6-cyl. 102×108 mm, 5250 cc (4″×4¼″, 320.4 cu.in.)

"Eight," 1939, 4-cyl. 56×100 mm, 1009 cc (2⅛″×4″, 61 cu.in.)

After 1947 production again became "standard" and concentrated on the "Vanguard." A new "Eight" and a "Ten" were later added.

"Vanguard," 1948, "standard" model, 4-cyl. 85×92 mm, 2088 cc (3¼″×3⅝″, 152 cu.in.)

"Ten," 1954
4-cyl. 63×76 mm, 948 cc (2½″×3″, 57.8 cu.in.)

In 1887 *John Marston,* an enamel and tinware manu-facturer, established the *Sunbeamland* cycle works, so called from his "japanned" goods. One or two cars were built in 1899, modeled on French de-signs. Production began in 1901 with the *Sunbeam-Mabley.*

Sunbeam-Mabley
1901

"12/16," 1915

4-cyl. 80×150 mm, 3016 cc (3⅛"×6", 184 cu.in.), descended from a more conventional range made from 1903 and copied from the *Berliet.*

1-cyl. 74×76 mm, 327 cc (2⅞"×3", 20 cu.in.), a "Victorian sofa," fitted with a wheel at each end and one at each side.

"3-liter," 1926

6-cyl. 75×110 mm, 2916 cc (3"×4⅜", 177.8 cu.in.) twin o.h.c.; based on the abundant racing experience of *Sunbeam-Talbot-Darracq.*

"Speed Model," 1934
6-cyl. 75×110 mm, 2916 cc
(3"×4⅜", 177.8
cu.in.)

Sunbeam Talbot "Ten," 1939, a dressed-up Hillman.

Adolphe Clément and *Lord Shrewsbury & Talbot* set up the Anglo-French firm of *Clément-Talbot* in 1903. It joined forces with *Darracq* in 1919, and in 1920 Sunbeam entered the combine, thereafter known as *Sunbeam-Talbot-Darracq* until the Rootes brothers bought out the British makes in 1935.

"90 Mk IIA"
1952

4-cyl. 81×110 mm, 2267 cc (3⅛"×4⅜", 138.2 cu.in.), the result of practical production arrangements (*Hillman* chassis and valve-in-head version of *Humber* "Hawk" mo-tor) plus rally experience. Won the 1953 Monte Carlo.

"Alpine," 1960
4-cyl. 81.5×76.2 mm, 1592 cc
(3⅛"×3", 97.1 cu.in.)

Great Britain

"Ten," 1923
4-cyl. 63.5 × 110 mm, 1393 cc (2½″ × 4⅜″, 85.1 cu. in.)

"14-60 hp Dolomite"
1938, 4-cyl. 75 × 100 mm, 1767 cc (3″ × 4″, 108 cu. in.)
The first *Triumph* cars were economy models, although fitted with hydraulic brakes from 1925. Later types varied from prosaic models to flagrant copies of the *Alfa Romeo*. After a few years as the "de luxe" edition of the Standard the marque made a comeback with the TR sports cars, based on Standard components. The "Herald" is notable for having independent rear suspension.

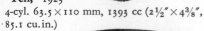

"Renown," 1950
(Standard "Vanguard" motor)

"Roadster," 1949
("Vanguard" motor)

"Mayflower," 1951, 4-cyl.
63 × 100 mm, 1247 cc
(2½″ × 4″, 76.3 cu. in.)

"TR 2," 1954
(modified "Vanguard" motor)

Triumph's history goes back to cycles and motorcycles; cars have been produced since 1923. It was taken over by *Standard* in 1945, and *Standard-Triumph International* was in turn taken over by *Leyland* in 1961.

"Herald 1200," 1961
4-cyl. 69.3 × 76 mm, 1147 cc
(2¾″ × 3″, 69.9 cu. in.)

Turner "Climax Sports," 1960, also available with a modified BMC "A" 948 cc (57 cu. in.) motor used in Morris, Austin, etc.

Vauxhall's ancestry goes back farther than that of any other make of car. When *William the Conqueror* invaded Britain in 1066, his followers included a trusty vassal by the name of *Fulke le Bréant*. He received an estate known as *Fulke's Hall*, a name which over the years became corrupted to Vauxhall, and centuries later the *Vauxhall Iron Works* was erected on land formerly belonging to this estate. They made marine engines and, in 1903, their first car. Two years later the works moved to Luton, where they are today. Since 1926 Vauxhall has belonged to *General Motors*.

1903, 1-cyl.
101.6 × 119.6 mm, 970 cc
(4″ × 4¾″, 59 cu. in.)

The badge was designed by *H. F. Varley*, and shows the griffon from the arms of Fulke le Bréant. The flutes along the bonnet — of which only a vestige now remains — were due to the make's chief engineer until 1922, *Laurence Pomeroy* senior.

"Prince Henry," 1911
4-cyl. 90 × 120 mm, 3054 cc (3⅝″ × 4¾″, 186 cu. in.); developed through participation in the Prince Henry trials.

"23/60 OD," 1923, 4-cyl. 95 × 140 mm, 3969 cc (3¾″ × 5½″, 243 cu. in.). Touring edition of the sports model "30/98 OE."

'Cadet' 1931

'Velox' 1949

'Velox' 1953

"Victor," 1957

"Cresta," 1960

"Tri-car," 1895-96
2-cyl. 79.4×127 mm, 1255 cc
(3⅛″×5″, 77 cu.in.)

"6hp," 1904
1-cyl. 114.2×127 mm, 1302 cc (4½″×5″, 79.5 cu.in.)

As the name *Wolseley Sheep Shearing Machine Co.* suggests, the company originally knew more about sheep-shearing than it did about motorcars. The same was true of the young technician *Herbert Austin,* who designed their first experimental model in 1895. The first 4-wheeled Wolseley came four years later. Austin left Wolseley to start on his own in 1905. His colleague *J. D. Siddeley* produced the *Wolseley-Siddeley* for the factory, which had been taken over by *Vickers* in 1901. The make came under Nuffield in 1927, and now belongs to BMC.

"3 hp'" 1899, 1-cyl. 114.2×127 mm, 1302 cc
(4½″×5″, 79.5 cu.in.)

"18/85," 1945

"15/60," 1959, alias BMC 1500 cc ADO 9

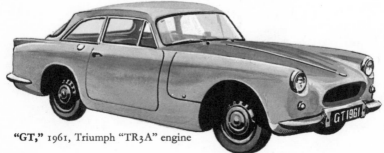

"GT," 1961, Triumph "TR3A" engine

The *Warwick* appeared in 1958 as the *Peerless,* and had links with the *Gordon.* The design used "TR2" components, including the engine, in a highly original chassis. The coachwork was fiberglass reinforced plastic.

Alta "1100 s/c"
1933-34

4-cyl. 60×95 mm, 1074 cc (2⅜″×3¾″, 65 cu.in.) supercharged; a few examples were built by *Geoffrey Taylor*.

Angus-Sanderson, 1920

The British car industry has known many makes now dead and gone. Some made their passing show in comparative silence, others were bright shooting stars, while a few sowed golden seeds for a crop of technical knowledge to be reaped in later years. The Scottish makes, such as *Argyll* and *Arrol-Johnston,* foundered through a combination of technical and financial blunders, and world trading conditions finally killed them off.

Argyll, 1903, 2-cyl. 88×140 mm, 1700 cc (3½″×5½″, 104 cu.in.) *Aster* engine

Siddeley, 1903   2-cyl. 114.3 × 114.3 mm, 2360 cc (4½″×4½″, 143.2 cu.in.)

In 1910 the make became the *Siddeley-Deasy,* and in 1919 joined *Armstrong-Whitworth*. It came under control of *Hawker* aircraft in 1935, was amalgamated with *Bristol* in 1959, and disappeared in 1960.

Armstrong-Siddeley
"Sapphire," 1953

Arrol-Johnston
1911

Belsize Bradshaw, 1922
2-cyl. 85×114 mm, 1200 cc (3¼″×4½″, 74 cu.in.)

This car, with an oil-cooled engine, was designed by the talented engineer *Granville Bradshaw* for the *Belsize* factory, which was active in the automobile industry from 1896-1926.

British Salmson, 1938

Brough Superior, 1937

BSA 'Scout' 1939

After a 3-wheeler, BSA made the front-wheel-drive "Scout" 1935-40.

Burney, 1930

The airship designer *Sir Dennis Burney* built a few streamlined rear-engined automobiles from 1930-33.

Calcott "10.5 hp," 1913

4-cyl. 65 × 110 mm, 1460 cc (2½″ × 4⅜″, 89 cu. in.). This make was made 1912-26, and was better than average.

Clyno "10.8 hp," 1926

4-cyl. 66 × 100 mm, 1368 cc (2⅝″ × 4″, 83 cu. in.), from the *Clyno Engineering Co. Ltd.,* which from 1922-29 built small cars in competition with Morris, but went under.

The *G. N.,* named after *H. R. Godfrey* and *Archibald Frazer-Nash,* was an unusually sporting "cyclecar," which led to the *Frazer-Nash* and the *H.R.G.*

Crossley "Shelsley," 1914

4-cyl. 80 × 130 mm, 2614 cc (3⅛″ × 5⅛″, 160 cu. in.). Passenger cars 1904-37. A chaotic production and sales policy hastened its end.

GWK, 1914

Air-cooled
2-cyl. engine
84 × 87 mm
1087 cc
(3¼″ × 3½″,
67 cu. in.)

G. N. "Touring"
1922

2-cyl. 86 × 90 mm, 1240 cc (3⅜″ × 3⅝″, 76.5 cu. in.), infinitely variable friction transmission. *Grice, Wood,* and *Keiller* were behind this light car which, with intervals and changes, was marketed 1911-32.

H. E. "16/55,"
1928

6-cyl. 65×115 mm, 2290 cc (2½″×4½″, 140 cu.in.). Between 1920 and 1931 the *Herbert Engineering Co.* built charming automobiles of differing types.

Horstman, 1921

4-cyl. 65×100 mm, 1327 cc (2½″×4″, 81 cu.in.) with a highly individual specification, including a kickstarter. Produced 1914-29 by *Sidney Horstmann*.

H. R. G. "1500,"
1948

4 c-cyl. 68×103 mm, 1496 cc (2⅝″×4⅛″, 91.5 cu.in.), a well-built, traditional sports car made by *Halford, Robins & Godfrey* 1935-56.

Invicta "4½-liter," 1935

6-cyl. 88.5×120 mm, 4467 cc (3½″×4¾″, 273 cu.in.)

Jowett "Standard Sedan,"
1936

4-cyl. 75.4×101.5 mm, 907 cc (3″×4″, 55 cu.in.) *Benjamin* and *William Jowett*'s indestructible twin-cylinder engine powered a very popular car. A 4-cyl. model appeared in 1936, and the sensational "Javelin" of 1947 also had a "flat four" (72.5×90 mm, 1486 cc; 2⅞″×3⅝″, 91 cu.in.). Production ceased in 1954, when the supply of bodies failed.

Jowett "Jupiter R4,"
1954

The make's last sports model, which never went into series-production.

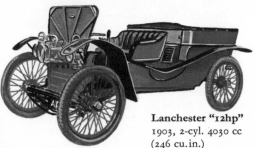

Lanchester "Dauphin," 1953

A disguised *Daimler*, although *Frederick William Lanchester* also carried out original and exceptional pioneering work. Daimler took over the make in 1931, and the name disappeared in 1956.

Lanchester "12hp"
1903, 2-cyl. 4030 cc
(246 cu.in.)

143

Great Britain

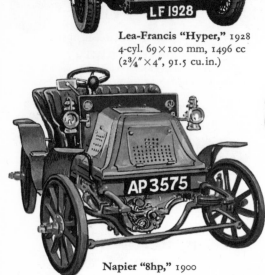

Lea-Francis "Hyper," 1928
4-cyl. 69×100 mm, 1496 cc
(2¾″×4″, 91.5 cu.in.)

Leyland "Eight," 1921
8-cyl. 89×146 mm, 7266 cc (3½″×5⅞″, 442.6
cu.in.), designed by *J. G. Parry-Thomas*; 16 were
built.

Napier "40/50," 1922
6-cyl. 101.6×127 mm, 6100 cc (4″×5″, 377 cu.in.);
Montague Napier was the engineer behind this big
car, which was in production until 1924.

Napier "8hp," 1900
2-cyl. 101.6×152.4 mm, 2470 cc (4″×6″, 151
cu.in.), the make's first series model, inspired by
Panhard & Levassor.

Railton, 1934

Terraplane 8 motor (8-cyl. 75×114 mm, 4010 cc;
3″×4½″, 245 cu.in.) and chassis were the basis
for *Reid A. Railton's* car, which had tremendous
acceleration and a respectable top speed. Made
1934-39 and, in very limited numbers, 1945-48.

North-Lucas, 1922

O. D. North used a 5-cyl. air-cooled radial engine
(70×76 mm, 1460 cc; 2¾″×3″, 89.5 cu.in.) and
independent suspension.

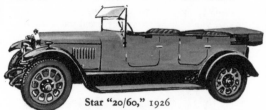

Star "20/60," 1926

6-cyl. 75×120 mm, 3180 cc (3″×4¾″, 194 cu.in.).
The factory originally made bicycles, but built
automobiles 1898-1932.

Adrian Squire produced a handful of very exciting
sports cars in 1935/36, using modified *Anzani*
motors (4-cyl. 69×100 mm, 1496 cc; 2¾″×4″,
91.5 cu.in.) with twin o.h.c. and a supercharger.

Squire, 1935

Straker-Squire "24/90," 1923

6-cyl. 80 × 130 mm, 3921 cc ($3\frac{1}{8}'' \times 5\frac{1}{8}''$, 239 cu.in.). Made 1908-26.

Stephens, 1898, 2-cyl. 77.8 × 152.4 mm, 1430 cc ($3\frac{1}{8}'' \times 6''$, 87 cu.in.)

The *Stephens* used a crude form of i.f.s. before the turn of the century. *Talbot* models of the Roesch period exhibited extreme technical refinement; the same was true of the *Straker-Squire,* while the *Swift* represented the solid, medium-class car. The *Wilson-Pilcher* had a preselector gearbox. *Edward Tamplin*'s automobiles were unorthodox, economy designs and the *Vale Special* was the Austin Healy "Sprite" of its time. *Leslie Hounsfield* gave the *Trojan* such a simplified, straightforward design that upkeep and running costs were reduced to the absolute minimum.

Swift "Cheylesmore," 1925

The former bicycle plant produced cars 1899-1931.

Tamplin, 1921
2-cyl. 85 × 85 mm, 900 cc ($3\frac{1}{4}'' \times 3\frac{1}{4}''$, 55 cu.in.); an interesting "cyclecar."

Talbot "105," 1934

6-cyl. 75 × 112 mm, 2976 cc ($3'' \times 4\frac{3}{8}''$, 181.5 cu.in.) designed by *Georges Roesch,* chief engineer from 1925-34.

Trojan, 1923, 2-cyl. 63.5 × 120.6 mm, 1527 cc ($2\frac{1}{2}'' \times 4\frac{3}{4}''$, 93.5 cu.in.) two-cycle engine.

Wilson-Pilcher, 1904

Vale Special, 1933

Italy

The Italian car industry has a proud ancestry. During the 15th-17th centuries talented men like *Valturio, Leonardo da Vinci, Ramelli,* and *Giovanni Branca* were tackling the technical problems of mechanical vehicles, although the first successful design—a steam carriage modeled on British lines—was by *Virginio Bordino* in 1854. It stands, with many other important cars, in the splendid Museo dell'Automobile at Turin. Italian designers had no success during the early development of internal-combustion engines and cars, although *Enrico Bernardi* and *Michele Lanza* each built a noteworthy motorcar in 1895. Professor Bernardi was an adventurous mechanical genius, while Lanza, an industrialist, was a romanticist with a practical turn of mind. From such different beginnings, they each eventually evolved a motorcar. Others carried on the work, and in spite of restrictive legislation the car forced its way onto the roads of Italy to become a national passion once the bastions of conservatism had been broken down. Both professional engineers and talented amateurs took to the car with infectious enthusiasm. Italian cars are built in a felicitous combination of favorable geographical circumstances, aesthetic traditions, and ardor for *una bella macchina*. This trait has been maintained as hand-production has given way to a large-scale industry, whose output has risen substantially in recent years to some 900,000 cars a year.

Michele Lanza (1868-1947) was a manufacturer of candles but built engines as a hobby. In 1895 he designed his first car (*right*) which was built in *Giovanni Martina*'s machinery works. It was followed by 12 other cars before he gave up, refusing an offer of partnership with *Giovanni Agnelli* who, a few years later, became one of the founders of *Fiat.*

Lanza, 1895

Boano body (1955) on an Alfa Romeo "1900 SS" chassis, an exquisite combination of engineering and styling.

A mercurial but quite continuous process of development separates Lanza's crude motor carriage and the Italian cars of today. The pioneers were faced with such basic, elementary problems that even to produce a design was a real challenge. They were succeeded by industrialists who were able to fit engineers' designs into a factory-production framework. Later came technical progress through racing, and finally the industry graduated to the fields of artistic achievement by fitting special coachwork (like that of Boano, *at left*) to well-designed chassis and engines.

146

Abarth "103," 1955
with modified
Fiat "1100" engine

Carlo Abarth, whose
Austrian forebears emigrated
to Italy, was one of the engineers behind the
Cisitalia. When this make was passing through one
of its periodic financial crises Abarth left to manufacture special equipment (in particular exhaust
systems). His firm developed into a specialized
producer of super-high-performance cars based on
various makes (Fiat, Simca, Alfa Romeo, Porsche,
etc).

Abarth was born under the sign of Scorpio, and
uses this as his badge.

"1000 Bialbero," 1961; Fiat
"600D" engine bored out to 982
cc (59.9 cu.in.) with twin o.h.c.
and two twin-choke carburetors;
93 bhp at 7000 rpm, 100 mph plus.

"Le Mans" model, 1961: a Fiat "600" cylinder block modified to 847 cc (51.7 cu.in.) fitted with two o.h.
camshafts and placed in the rear of a space-frame chassis.

"1600," 1962, based on the Fiat "1500."

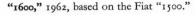

"850 GT," 1959
a much-modified
Fiat "600."

NICOLA ROMEO
1876-1938

A. L. F. A., 1909

"RM," 1925, 4-cyl.

76 × 110 mm, 1996 cc (3″ × 4⅜″, 121.5 cu. in.)
The "RLT" model of 1923 (6-cyl. 75 × 110 mm, 2916 cc; 3″ × 4⅜″, 177.8 cu. in.) was the starting-point for the "Tipo RLS" (6-cyl. 76 × 110 mm, 2994 cc; 3″ × 4⅜″, 182.5 cu. in.), and "RM." It was further developed to produce a "Targa Florio" model with a slightly larger and more rugged engine, and the "RLSS"; the latter was Alfa Romeo's series sports car until the Jano motors came into production.

In 1906 the French automobile industry pioneer, *Alexandre Darracq,* set up an assembly plant in Naples and another on the outskirts of Milan. Neither flourished, and in 1909 both were taken over by an Italian group. Activity was then concentrated at Milan (Portello), and the firm was given the title *Anonima Lombardo Fabbrica Automobili,* commonly shortened to A.L.F.A. The factory lived on foreign designs and bank loans; this basis of operation was untenable, and the main creditor, the *Banca di Sconto,* called in a young railway engineer named *Nicola Romeo* who managed wartime production from 1915-18 and carried out a reorganization in 1919; this led to the name of *Alfa Romeo,* and a range of very attractive cars. The firm won fame on the racing circuits; A.L.F.A. had been racing as early as 1911-14, and continued after 1918 with improved versions of the 1914 racing model (4-cyl. 100 × 143 mm, 4500 cc; 4″ × 5⅝″, 275 cu. in.). The "RLS" of 1923 was the first sports car, and after an unsuccessful GP car (the "P1") the classic "P2" followed in 1923, designed by *Vittorio Jano.* This had an 8-cyl. supercharged twin o.h.c. engine (61 × 85 mm, 1987 cc; 2⅜″ × 3¼″, 121.5 cu. in.).

"RLSS," 1927

6-cyl. 76 × 110 mm, 2994 cc (3″ × 4⅜″, 182.5 cu. in.), pushrod o.h.v., 83 bhp

In 1926 a 1½-liter (91.5 cu. in.) model appeared, with a single o.h. camshaft; the following year saw the twin o.h.c. version and 1929 a twin o.h.c. sports car (6-cyl. 65 × 88 mm, 1750 cc; 2⅝″ × 3½″, 108 cu. in.); also available with a supercharger.

"6 C 1750," 1930

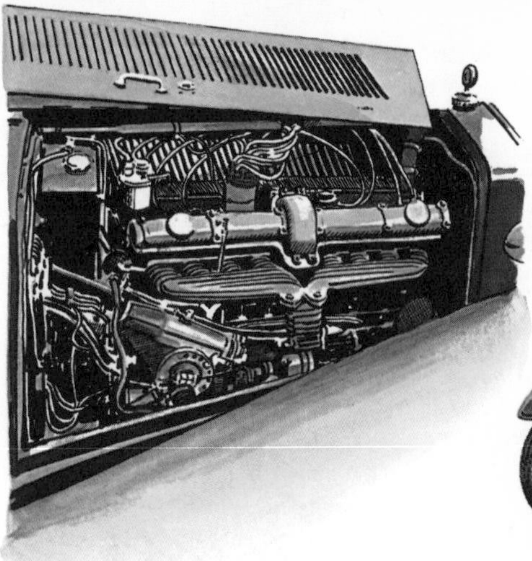

"8 C 2300," 1932

The Crusaders from Milan bore a snake on their banners, shown swallowing a Saracen to commemorate their victories. The cross symbolizes the delivery of Jerusalem.

"8 C 2300," 1932

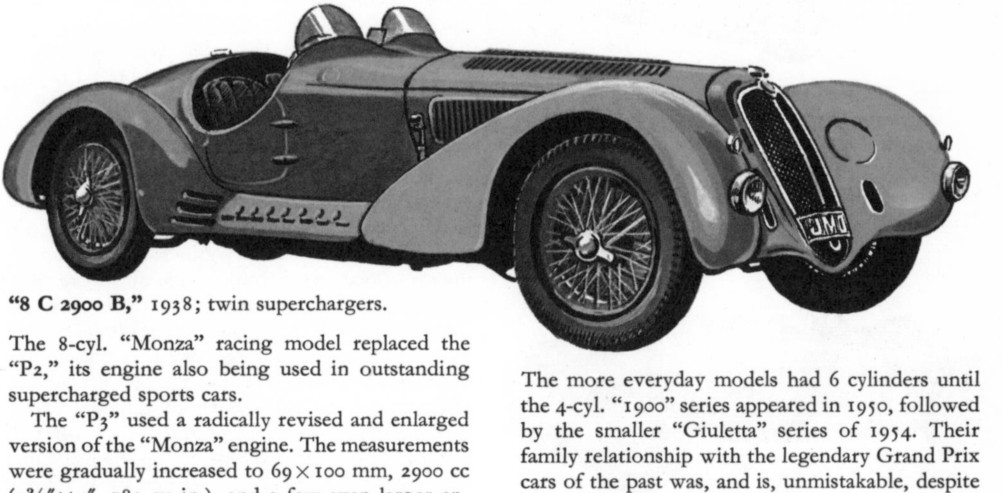

"8 C 2300," 1932

"8 C 2900 B," 1938; twin superchargers.

The 8-cyl. "Monza" racing model replaced the "P2," its engine also being used in outstanding supercharged sports cars.

The "P3" used a radically revised and enlarged version of the "Monza" engine. The measurements were gradually increased to 69×100 mm, 2900 cc ($2\frac{3}{4}'' \times 4''$, 182 cu. in.), and a few even larger engines were made. When it became obsolete for GP racing, those remaining in stock were used in the fascinating "8 C 2900 B."

The more everyday models had 6 cylinders until the 4-cyl. "1900" series appeared in 1950, followed by the smaller "Giuletta" series of 1954. Their family relationship with the legendary Grand Prix cars of the past was, and is, unmistakable, despite the more industrialized production and design.

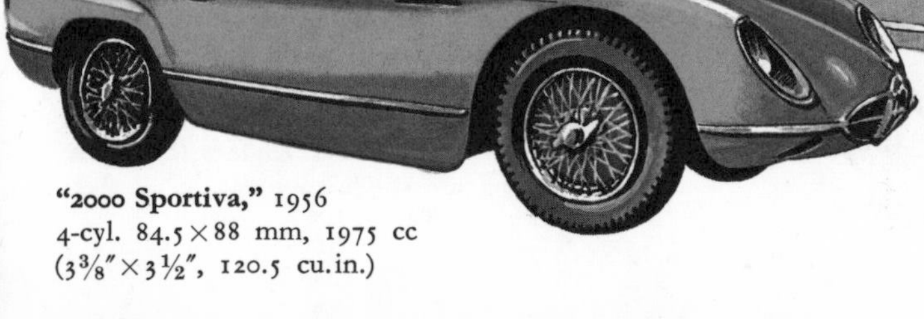

"2000 Sportiva," 1956
4-cyl. 84.5×88 mm, 1975 cc
($3\frac{3}{8}'' \times 3\frac{1}{2}''$, 120.5 cu. in.)

"Giulietta Sprint," 1959
4-cyl. 74×75 mm, 1290 cc
($3'' \times 3''$, 78.7 cu. in.)

149

Ferrari "Tipo 815," 1940

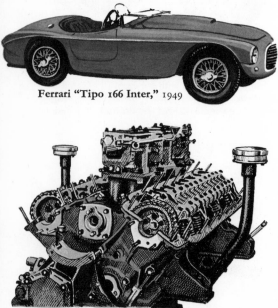

Ferrari "Tipo 125," 1947

ENZO FERRARI

The first "Ferrari" cars were really modified Alfa Romeo racing cars made for *Scuderia Ferrari,* including the frightening "Bimotore" of 1935 with an engine at each end. The "Tipo 815" was designed for the 1940 Mille Miglia, using two modified Fiat "1100" engines as the basis for a 1½-liter (91.5 cu. in.) straight-8, which was installed in a light tubular chassis.

Ferrari "Tipo 166 Inter," 1949

At Maranello, some 9 miles outside Modena, stands the factory set up by *Enzo Ferrari* when Alfa Romeo could no longer supply "Scuderia Ferrari" with race-winning cars. Ferrari had been a racing driver since his young days, and when he ceased to compete actively in 1931 Alfa Romeo were on the point of giving up factory participation in racing. There was no connection between the two events, but they became linked when Ferrari organized his racing "stable," recruiting the best drivers of the day and prevailing on Alfa Romeo to supply the cars. "Scuderia Ferrari" swept all before it in 1933, but then lost so much ground to the Government-supported German makes that Ferrari decided to build his own cars. The war spoiled his plans, and it was not until 1947 that a purely Ferrari car could make its debut. The design came from *Gioachino Colombo,* the designer responsible for the famous 1½-liter Alfa Romeo, "Tipo 158," and the new Ferrari incorporated every possible refinement. It had a V-12 engine, although the design purported to be intended only for a 1500 cc (91.5 cu. in.) sports car. It soon became obvious that a parallel production of sports, racing, and luxury cars was the intention—with a marked similarity in design. The type numbers are derived from the capacity of the individual cylinders of the engine.

Ferrari used exclusively 12-cyl. engines up to 1951, when Colombo's successor, *Aurelio Lampredi,* brought out a 4-cyl. racing car after having worked wonders with the big 4½-liter (275 cu. in.) 12-cyl. engine which finally broke the dominance of Alfa Romeo in 1951. The 12-cyl. engines (*left*) were continued, and are still used today in all their awe-inspiring complexity.

"Tipo 340," 1952, "America"
Vignale coachwork.

Early bodies were strictly functional. Later, the
creazioni of leading Italian designers were used to
adorn the Ferrari chassis.

A 6-cyl. in-line engine was added
to the 12- and 4-cyl. models in
1954. Work was already under
way on a V-6 in 1950, and the
latest racing Ferraris have V-6s.

"Tipo 250, Testa Rossa" sports car, 1958, with
Scaglietti body.

The "Scuderia Ferrari" emblem is the coal-black
prancing horse of Ravenna on a yellow background. It is from the arms of the Baracca family
who consented to its use in memory of their son
killed while flying during the 1914-18 war.

Automobili Ferrari took over the racing team's
emblem as its radiator badge, and in 1960 Enzo
Ferrari's autocratic organization was made into a
limited company, *Società Esercizio Fabbricazione
Automobile e Corse,* which now carries on the work
of its founder.

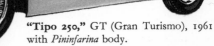

"Tipo 250," GT (Gran Turismo), 1961
with *Pininfarina* body.

F. I. A. T., 1899

The first rear-engined F. I. A. T. models bore the stamp of German designs. After 1901 more functional French patterns were followed.

F. I. A. T., 1900

The twin-cyl. rear-engined models were replaced in 1901 by cars with a 4-cyl. engine at the front.

"24 CV," 1906

Giovanni Agnelli (1866-1945) had exceptional foresight and made good use of influential connections when, in 1899, he founded the *Società Italiana per la Costruzione e il Commercio delle Automobili Torino;* this unwieldy title was changed soon after to *Fabbrica Italiana Automobili Torino,* and their technical director *Aristide Faccioli* suggested using the initials as a trade name. The present name of *Fiat* was registered in 1906.

Energetic participation in racing and close collaboration between the technical and commercial sides of the management built up a powerful industrial group which absorbed a number of makes, and today produces some 80% of all Italian automobiles. Fiat's field of activity gradually spread far beyond cars alone, and covers land, sea, and air—as expressed in their proud motto *"Terra-Mare-Cielo."*

The factory's technical experience was soon employed on the series-production of "bread-and-butter" cars, and the famous "Zero" series was introduced in 1912. Innumerable examples of this rugged car were made 1912-1915.

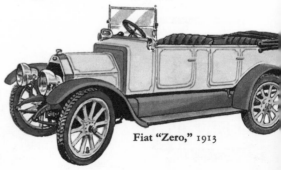

Fiat "Zero," 1913

Fiat "501," 1923
4-cyl. 65×110 mm, 1460 cc ($2\frac{5}{8}'' \times 4\frac{3}{8}''$, 89.5 cu. in.)

Although he was trained for the Law, *Carlo Cavalli* was such an outstanding engineer that he was able, in 1917, to take over the technical management of Fiat. His designs struck a balance between stolid common sense and flashes of brilliance, and in the "501" he founded a tradition which Fiat has followed ever since—family cars with properties derived from the dizzy, hairpin roads of the Alps, and which now and then hint at their proud past on the racing circuits.

The unusually well-balanced "501" was made 1919-26. The "509" (o. h. v. 990 cc engine, 57×97 mm; 60 cu. in., $2\frac{1}{4}'' \times 3\frac{7}{8}''$) which replaced it was the forerunner of the "Balilla" series, which in 1938 became the "Millecento" (i.e. 1100).

"Balilla 508S," 1934

In standard form the "Balilla" was quite sedate, but a lightweight body and a valve-in-head motor produced a very spirited car.

"500 C," 1949

The last of the "Topolino" series, begun by *Dante Giacosa* with his "500" model in 1936.

"1100 S," 1946
With i. f. s. and a new engine the "Balilla" became the "Millecento" in 1938, and again combined economy with verve, especially when fitted with a lightweight, streamlined body. Chassisless construction was introduced in 1953.

"8-V" sports, 1952
(1996 cc, 72×61.3 mm;
121.8 cu. in., $2\frac{7}{8}'' \times 2\frac{1}{2}''$),
limited production for a few years.

"Millecento," 1959
(4-cyl. 68×75 mm, 1089 cc;
$2\frac{5}{8}'' \times 3''$, 67 cu. in.)

"1500," 1962

Italy

The important industrial concern of *Innocenti,* Milan (makers of *Lambretta* scooters) took up license production of the Austin "A40" in 1960. The same year at Turin they showed their version of the *Austin-Healey* "Sprite" (p. 117), the chassis and engine wearing bodywork by *Officine Stapaggi Industriale,* a firm founded by *Fergat* and *Ghia.*

Innocenti "950"
British "works" in
an Italian body

Lancia "Alpha," 1909

The early Lancias were noted for clean design and exquisite detail workmanship.

Vincenzo Lancia (1881-1937) was a racing and test driver for *Fiat* when, in 1907, he joined up with *Claudio Fogolin* to form *Lancia & C.* and to build cars after his own ideas. The first Lancia appeared in 1908, and was a very elegant lightweight design. Tentative experiments with i.f.s. were made as early as 1910, and a sensational 12-cyl. model with the cylinders at an angle of 20 degrees was seen in 1919. The "Kappa" series was still quite orthodox in design, but in the "Lambda" series of 1922 Lancia introduced such novel features as a V-4 engine, i.f.s. with coil springs and unit construction of chassis and body.

"Kappa," 1919

4-cyl. 110×130 mm, 4940 cc (4⅜″×5⅛″, 301 cu.in.): a sober, well-built car with handling well above the average for its day.

The radiator badge was designed by *Carlo Biscaretti di Ruffia,* founder of the Turin Motor Museum.

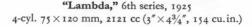

"Lambda," 6th series, 1925
4-cyl. 75×120 mm, 2121 cc (3″×4¾″, 154 cu.in.)

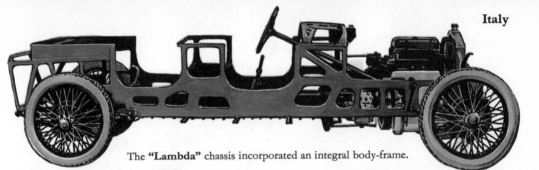

The **"Lambda"** chassis incorporated an integral body-frame.

The distinctive "Lambda" specification was seen again in the 8-cyl. series which began with the "Dilambda," and its smaller companion, the "Astura" of 1931. The 4-cyl. "Artena," "Aprilia," "Ardea," and "Appia" all have the same features.

"Appia" engine, 10° V-4, 68×75 mm, 1090 cc (2¾"×3", 67 cu.in.), brought out in 1953. Every inch a Lancia design: compact, accessible, with beautiful castings and careful detail finish throughout.

"Aprilia," 1937
V-4, 72×83 mm, 1350 cc (2⅞"×3¼", 82 cu.in.), integral body-frame.

The "Ardea" (V-4, 65×68 mm, 903 cc; 2⅝"×2¾", 82 cu.in.) was introduced in 1940, and continued in production until replaced by the "Appia" in 1953. In its final version the "Ardea" engine had an aluminum cylinder head, with a 5-speed transmission after 1948. The "Aurelia" series began in 1950 with the "B 10" (V-6, 70×76 mm, 1754 cc; 2¾"×3", 108 cu.in.) and in 1958 gave way to the "Flaminia" series, which dropped the classic Lancia front suspension.

"Aurelia GT," 1953
2451 cc, V-6 78×85.5 mm (3⅛"×3¼", 149.5 cu.in.)

The "Flavia," launched in 1960, has a flat-four engine and is not a Lancia design; it was planned in 1948 by *Prof. Fessia* as the *Cemsa-Caproni* (p. 161).

"Flavia," 1961

"Sedici cilindri," 1932, *Zagato* body

The god Neptune stirred the waters with his trident, bringing forth tempest and earthquake—which makes any further explanation of the *Maserati* emblem superfluous!

The beginning of the *Officine Alfieri Maserati* are to be found in five brothers' passionate interest in engines. More precisely, they can be traced back to the tiny auxiliary motor which *Carlo Maserati* fitted to a bicycle in 1898. From then on the activities of Carlo and his younger brothers can be followed in firms such as *Fiat, Bianchi, Isotta-Fraschini, Junior,* and *Diatto* until, in 1925, *Bindo, Alfieri, Ettore,* and *Ernesto* started up a family business under the sign of the trident.

The first Maserati (1926) was an 8-cyl. 1½-liter (91 cu.in.) racing car with a superb engine made like a fine watch, and from then on the marque produced cars purely for racing purposes. Limited production made frequent changes of model possible, and up to 1939 there were scarcely two identical cars from the *Casa del tridente.* Their wins were legion throughout the world, and Maserati alone of the European makes has won the Indianapolis "500" race twice under modern conditions (*Wilbur Shaw* in 1939 and 1940). Their sports cars were thinly disguised Grand Prix models, and most of them for that reason had quite small motors; however, the fierce "Sedici cilindri" with its two 8-cyl. supercharged engines side-by-side was quite awe-inspiring, and the "Sei cilindri" which followed was no less impressive. Besides making cars Maserati also produced machine tools, and in 1939 the whole concern moved from Bologna to Modena.

In 1946 the brothers had to relinquish the family firm and name to the *Orsi* company, which continued the fine racing tradition. These efforts were crowned when *J. M. Fangio* won the Drivers' World Championship in 1957 in a Maserati "250/ Fr." Since then Maserati has given up making purely racing cars, to concentrate on sports and Gran Turismo models; technically these are closely akin to the victorious GP cars, and follow the ingenious paths of almost abstract engineering.

"Sei cilindri," 1934

"Tipo A6/1500," 1947

6-cyl. 66×82.5 mm, 1488 cc ($2\frac{5}{8}'' \times 3\frac{1}{4}''$, 91 cu. in.). This postwar model was the last Maserati before the brothers left to establish the new *OSCA* marque (p. 158).

"Tipo A6 GCS/2000," 1953

6-cyl. 76.5×72 mm, 1988 cc ($3'' \times 2\frac{7}{8}''$, 121.5 cu. in.), twin o.h.c.; designed for serious sports car racing.

"Gran Turismo 3000"
1956

"3500 GT," 1961
6-cyl. 86×100 mm, 3485 cc ($3\frac{3}{8}'' \times 4''$, 212 cu. in.)

"250/Fr," 1957
The catalogue car with a World Championship.

Italy

Moretti "1500 EGT"
1961
4-cyl. 79×75 mm, 1470 cc, twin o.h.c. (3⅛″×3″, 90.5 cu.in.)

During the twenties *Giovanni Moretti* started making motorcycles and electric delivery vans in Turin. The make's first passenger car was also electric, but was abandoned in 1946 while still in the experimental stage in favor of a twin-cyl. 350 cc (21 cu.in.) mini-car. This was superseded in 1948 by a 4-cyl. 700 cc (43 cu.in.) model, which grew to 750 cc (46 cu.in.) with one or two o.h. camshafts and correspondingly varying performance. Larger engines followed. The cars range from small cars of modest performance to out-and-out racing cars—the Moretti is made to order.

Nardi & Cia are another of the small Turin firms ready, at short notice, to produce almost any sort of car. Their production includes special steering wheels, engine conversions, bodywork, and whole cars to completely individual specifications. They made the first *Ferrari* ("Tipo 815," p. 150) to Enzo Ferrari's design. If the phrase "series-production" may be used at all in connection with Nardi cars, it must apply to the "Tipo 750" which is Fiat 600-based; all the same, individual specifications are the rule.

Nardi "750," 1950
fitted with 2-cyl. air-cooled BMW engine.

OSCA stands for *Officine Spezializzate Costruzioni Automobili,* founded in 1946 by the Maserati brothers.

OSCA "Mt 4—Corsa Sport," 1948

From the very first 1100 cc (67 cu.in.) OSCA of 1948, the Maserati brothers have pursued uncompromising technical ideals. *Fiat* now fits its "1600S" convertible with detuned OSCA engines.

OSCA "1500 tipo promiscuo," 1958
4-cyl. 78×78 mm, 1491 cc (3⅛″×3⅛″, 91.5 cu.in.), "mixed model," i.e. a combined sports-racing car.

Every OSCA is of racing-car design, detuned to suit the client's wishes and needs, or prepared to give the ultimate in performance.

OSCA "1600 GT," 1961
Zagato body

As the name implies the *Società Auto Trasformazioni Accessori*—SIATA for short—deals with the conversion and modification of production cars and makes special accessories. This firm, too, is based in Turin, and has used mainly *Fiat* motors. *Siata-Abarth S. p. A* was formed in 1959 and has, with technical assistance from *Abarth* (p. 147) and financial backing by Fiat, taken over the manufacture of Fiat variants, commercial vehicles, etc., while Abarth carries on its own production of cars and special equipment.

Siata
with Fiat 8-V motor, 1952

Stanguellini "Bialbero 750," 1950

Vittorio Stanguellini played with cars from his cradle, and he was not satisfied with just running an ordinary Fiat dealer's business in Modena. In 1935 he opened a special department to carry out *"elaborazioni"* on family cars, with incredible results. Gradually quite a few cars with heavily modified Fiat power units left his workshop, and in time their individuality became so marked that the new *Stanguellini* marque was established. The engines are still Fiat-based, although nothing but a modified cylinder block remains—the rest is a finely engineered racing unit: twin o.h. camshafts, special inlet and exhaust systems, etc., and tubular chassis with highly developed suspension.

Neither inside nor out did this or any of the subsequent 750 cc (46 cu. in.) Stanguellini models seem to have anything in common with their sedate Fiat origins. The same applies to the 1100 cc (67 cu. in.) cars.

Stanguellini "Junior," 1961

"Formula Junior" was an Italian-inspired attempt to create a low-cost racing class based on production engines. Stanguellini used a modified Fiat "1100" engine, with twin-choke Weber carburetors.

Italy has many vanished makes. Together they form a mosaic pattern of the buoyant plans of little firms and the more-or-less serious flirtations between big industrial groups and the unnamed Muse of the motor-engineering world. Every closed chapter in the highly colored history of the Italian motorcar industry recalls an irrepressible creative urge which sometimes, by sheer enthusiasm, rose above financial or technical limitations.

Ansaldo "4A," 1925
4-cyl. 70 × 120 mm, 1850 cc
(2¾″ × 4¾″, 112.5 cu.in.)

This make was produced 1920-31 by the big Ansaldo company, which is still very active in heavy engineering. It was a restrained design, but held several international class records during the twenties.

Ansaldo "Tipo 18," 1930

6-cyl. 75 × 105 mm, 2780 cc (3″ × 4⅛″, 169 cu.in.), o.h.v., single o.h. camshaft, 4-speed transmission.

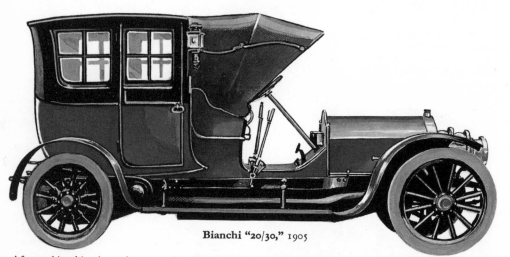

Bianchi "20/30," 1905

After making bicycles and motorcycles, *Edoardo Bianchi* built cars, but in recent years their passenger cars have been limited to modified Fiat models.

Ceirano "Tipo S 150," 1925
4-cyl. 65 × 110 mm, 1460 cc
(2⅝″ × 4⅜″, 89.5 cu.in.)

Giovanni and *Matteo Ceirano* produced "Welleyes" cycles around the start of the century, and built a "Welleyes" car in 1898/99. The entire firm, whose staff included *Faccioli* and *Lancia,* was taken over by FIAT, but the Ceirano brothers soon resumed business on their own. For a while the name SCAT (Società Ceirano Automobili Torino, see p. 164) was used for a subsidiary. The firm eventually passed to Fiat in the 1920s.

Cemsa-Caproni, 1948

Immediately after 1945 there were plans for using the idle production capacity of the *Caproni* aircraft factory for making cars. A distinctive prototype designed by *Prof. Fessia* was launched in 1948 as the *Cemsa-Caproni,* but the project was abandoned. It had a specification unusual for its time, with a 1100 cc (67 cu.in.) flat-four motor, front-wheel drive, a platform chassis, and independent suspension all around. It reappeared as the *Minerva* in 1953, but only went into production in 1960 as the *Lancia* "Flavia."

Chiribiri, 1923

During the 1920s *Deo Chiribiri* built light touring, sports, and racing cars, driven amongst others by *Tazio Nuvolari.*

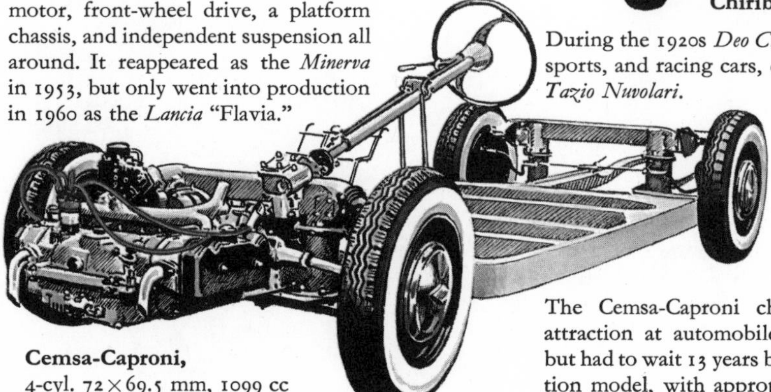

Cemsa-Caproni,
4-cyl. 72 × 69.5 mm, 1099 cc
(2⅞″ × 2¾″, 67 cu.in.)

The Cemsa-Caproni chassis was a prominent attraction at automobile shows during 1947-48, but had to wait 13 years before becoming a production model, with appropriate design changes.

Italy

Piero Dusio, a textile manufacturer, began producing automobiles in 1946 with 50 identical *Cisitalia* light racing cars, fitted with modified *Fiat* "1100" engines. These were followed by sports cars, by a four-wheel-drive GP model designed by Dr. Porsche—and by the inevitable bankruptcy.

Cisitalia "202," 1948

Despite ruin, a stillborn Grand Prix car, and an unsuccessful attempt to establish Cisitalia in Argentina, Dusio reappears from time to time with fresh novelties. For a time modified marine motors from *Botta & Puricelli, Milan* were used; *Ford* engines and parts have been employed, but Fiat forms the staple basis.

Cisitalia "202 D,"
1952

During the First World War the *Diatto* company, which had been active since 1907, bought the license rights on an 8-cyl. *Bugatti* aero engine. The connection continued after the war, when the "Type 22" and "23" Bugattis and others were sold as Diatto cars; at the same time they were developing their own models, which later served as a starting point for *Maserati.* A whole slice of European automotive history is thus linked with the long-departed Diatto, which ceased manufacture in 1930.

Diatto "Tipo 35," 1925
4-cyl. 90 × 116 mm,
3000 cc
(3⅝″ × 4½″, 183 cu. in.)

Isotta-Fraschini, 1911
4-cyl.
130 × 150 mm,
8000 cc
(5⅛″ × 6″,
488 cu. in.)

At the end of the 1890s *Oreste Fraschini* went into partnership with *Cesare Isotta,* and the newly formed automobile factory became *Isotta-Fraschini.* With technical assistance from the big *De Dietrich* concern, the factory enjoyed the use of *Bugatti's* design talents while he was with De Dietrich. Apart, however, from an exquisite Bugatti-designed model Isotta-Fraschini kept to large cars, and are especially remembered for having introduced four-wheel brakes in 1910.

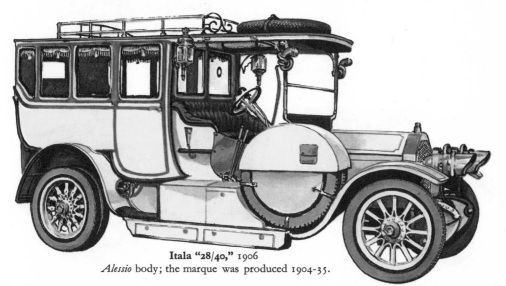

Isotta-Fraschini "Tipo 8A Spinto," 1929

"Monterosa," 1947

The "Tipo 8" introduced in 1919 gave way in the 1920s to the "Tipo 8A" (8-cyl. 95 × 130 mm, 7372 cc; $3\frac{3}{4}'' \times 5\frac{1}{8}''$, 450 cu.in.), and an improved "Tipo 8B" in 1933. With abundant engine power and a rugged chassis, the Isotta-Fraschini "8A" and "8B" were magnificent touring cars, much favored by custom coach-builders. The "Spinto" and "Super Spinto" variants, with rather more powerful motors, were fairly fast into the bargain. In 1947 the factory announced the revolutionary "Monterosa," with a 3.4 liter (210 cu.in.) V-8 rear engine and many technical refinements, but this was unsuited to the post war economic climate and in 1949 Isotta-Fraschini went into liquidation. As a result a gifted young engineer, *Aurelio Lampredi*, had to look for a new job, which he found with *Ferrari*. He later moved on to join *Fiat*.

Itala "28/40," 1906
Alessio body; the marque was produced 1904-35.

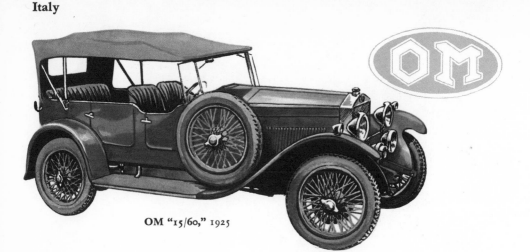

OM "15/60," 1925

Among the Italian sporting cars of the twenties, those from *Officine Meccaniche* occupy a special niche. Mechanically, they were an odd mixture of old-fashioned design, modern refinement, and painstaking production. The cars were fast, despite a L-head motor—they took the first three places in the 1927 Mille Miglia—but the engine details point to a high power output. The "15/60" was a 6-cyl. (65 × 100 mm, 1991 cc; $2\frac{5}{8}'' \times 4''$, 121.5 cu.in.). A supercharged model was available, and o.h. valves were listed as "extra equipment." No cars were made after 1934.

Prinetti e Stucchi began making motorcycles and light cars in Milan in 1898. They left no great mark on the car industry, but belong in the over-all picture as the plant where young *Ettore Bugatti* served his apprenticeship and first gave an indication of his mechanical genius with a twin-engined tricycle and a four-engined car. Perhaps these experiments persuaded the firm to devote itself entirely to the production of sewing machines.

Prinetti e Stucchi, 1899

SCAT stood for *Società Ceirano Automobili Torino* (see p. 161). This firm was in production from 1906-27, and gained sporting renown by winning the Targa Florio in 1911, 1912, and 1914.

SCAT, 1909, often confused with the French SCAP

SPA, 1921, with *Bertone* body

Società Ligure Piemontese Automobili used three of its initials as the trade name for a range of well-built cars which were in production from 1908. Sporting wins, including the Targa Florio in 1909, led to regular series-production, discontinued during the 1914-18 war. The models of the 1920s were a 6-cyl. 4½-liter (275 cu.in.) with a superb motor, and a 4-cyl. 2.7-liter (164 cu.in.) with a less convincing specification.

Temperino made a valiant attempt in the twenties to bring out an utterly simple but acceptable car design. A twin-cylinder 1200 cc (74 cu.in.) air-cooled motor was mounted in an uncomplicated chassis, and the bodywork was rather plain. The design was too crude to sustain production for any length of time.

Temperino, 1921
2-cyl. 1200 cc (74 cu.in.) air-cooled

The Swiss engineer *Roberto Züst* was the creator of the *Züst,* also called the *Brixia-Züst* (Brixia being the Latin name for Brescia). It was in production 1906-14, and is particularly remembered for its third place in the incredible "race" from New York to Paris (via Siberia) in 1908.

Züst "25/35," 1913
4-cyl. 100 × 150 mm, 4712 cc
(4" × 6", 287 cu.in.)

Japan

Nippon

The nationality plate is shown here in Japanese script, since Japan (Nippon) is not a signatory to the International Traffic Convention.

Japan's automobile industry began in 1907 with the *Takuri* cars and grew during the 1914-18 war, only to be paralyzed by the Tokyo earthquake of 1923. Motoring increased through imports and license production during the following years, and the 1930s saw independent Japanese manufacture, especially of models suitable for military use. The need for road transport after 1945 brought rapid development, and the annual production of cars is over 260,000.

Lila, 1923

The industrial concern *Jitsuyo Jidosha Seizo Co. Ltd.* built the light *Gorham* and *Lila* cars.

Takuri, 1907

Shintaro Yoshida and *Komanosuke Uchiyama* built the first Japanese automobile—albeit with an American engine—in 1902. Five years later they produced an entirely Japanese car, the *Takuri,* about ten of which were sold.

Ohtomo, 1925

Junya Toyokawa studied automobile engineering in the USA prior to 1917, and then set up *Hakuyosha & Co.* which built, among others, the air-cooled *Ohtomo.* The company crashed soon after.

Mitsubishi "A," 1918

The shipyard division of the *Mitsubishi* concern at Kobe produced cars experimentally 1917-21.

Datsun, 1932

Hino "Contessa," 1961

Hino Co. Ltd., a heavy engineering firm, makes the
Renault "4CV" under license, and in 1961 developed their own "Contessa" from the "Dauphine."
The engine is bored out for a slightly higher output, the final drive ratios are lower—and the "Contessa" is very ruggedly built to cope with local
conditions.

Mazda "R 360," 1961

Producing this light model in 1960, the Hiroshima
Toyo Kogyo works extended its manufacture of
light trucks to include passenger cars.

Datsun "Bluebird," 1960

In 1927 *Jitsuyo Jidosha Seizo* took over the
Kwaishinsha works, which had been established in 1912 and which made the *DAT* cars.
The name was changed in 1931 to *Datson,*
and in 1932 to *Datsun.* After a financial re-
shuffle the name was again altered to *Nissan*
in 1934, and the *Nissan Motor Co. Ltd.* now
produces Nissan
and Datsun
vehicles.

Mitsubishi "500," 1960

The reorganized Mitsubishi concern
supplemented its heavy engineering
output in 1960 with this small and well-
built automobile.

Prince "Skyline," 1962

Prince Motors Ltd. have their roots in the aircraft
industry, and their automobile designs show
distinctive detail
features.

Subaru "360," 1962

2-cyl. (61.5 × 60 mm, 356 cc; $2\frac{3}{8}'' \times 2\frac{3}{8}''$, 21.6
cu. in.) 2-cycle rear engine, made by *Fuji Heavy
Industries Ltd.* since 1958.

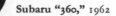

**Toyopet
"Crown,"** 1960

Irgens, c. 1897

Geographical and economic conditions precluded all attempts to establish a car industry in Norway, although Norwegian pioneers showed exceptional foresight, both technically and administratively.

Paul Henningsen Irgens (1843-1923), for example, built a marine engine in 1880 and designed an automobile in 1883, as well as patenting a gas turbine in 1898. A little earlier he built a car at Bergen. *Markus Hansen Fossum* produced cars between 1905-1907, and the *Norsk Automobil & Vognfabrik A/S* was founded in 1907 but never reached series-production. At times various assembly plants were active, without lasting success. *Anto Løvstad* anticipated a number of car designers with his remarkable patent of 1878 for torsion-bar springing on horse-drawn carriages.

Fossum, 1907

Norsk Automobil & Vognfabrik, 1908

Norwegian coach-builders assembled such makes as *Scania-Vabis, Chrysler, Rockne,* and *Dodge.* From the 1920s the *Geijer* was assembled from US parts, including a *Lycoming* motor. The German occupation 1940-45 put a stop to all Norwegian automobile assembly, and later attempts were abandoned.

Geijer, 1929

The Dutch have produced some ten different makes, among them the delightful *Spyker*. During the twenties competition from the large industrial nations became too fierce, although a comeback was made in 1958 when a highly interesting design was launched at the Amsterdam Show.

The *Spyker* occupies a place of honor in automotive history as the first make to use a 6-cyl. motor (1902); the 4-cyl. models were, however, far more popular.

Spyker, 1905
4-cyl. 90 × 100 mm, 2546 cc
($3\frac{5}{8}'' \times 4''$, 150 cu. in.)

The marque dates from 1900, and was in production until 1925. The last models, like that on the left, fitted *Maybach* motors (6-cyl. 95 × 135 mm, 5740 cc; $3\frac{3}{4}'' \times 5\frac{1}{4}''$, 350 cu. in.).

Spyker, 1924

DAF "Variomatic" (*below*); infinitely variable belt drive to the rear wheels. The effective diameter of the front pulleys is governed by the engine vacuum, that of the back pulleys by built-in bob-weights.

DAF "600," 1958

DAF "Variomatic" transmission

In 1958 *Van Dorne's Automobielfabriek* developed a light, air-cooled 2-cyl. car with an ingenious automatic transmission system giving infinitely variable gearing from 20:1 to 4.4:1. The clutch is an automatic centrifugal mechanism. A 750 cc (46 cu. in.) model (85.5 × 65 mm; $3\frac{3}{8}'' \times 2\frac{5}{8}''$), and the better-equipped "Daffodil" were introduced in 1961.

Poland – Argentina – China

The Mikrus "MR 300" has a twin-cyl. 298 cc (18 cu.in.) 2-cycle motor at the back driving the rear wheels, while the Syrena has a similar 744 cc (45.5 cu.in.) front engine driving the front wheels. The design brings early DKWs to mind. Both cars are intended exclusively for the home market.

Prior to 1939 there were few native Polish car manufacturers, but a number of foreign firms, notably General Motors and Fiat, had assembly plants in the country. After 1945 production of the *Warszawa* was begun, based on the Russian *Pobieda* which externally resembled the Standard "Vanguard." Since then two small cars have come into series-production, the *Mikrus* "MR 300" and *Syrena*. Annual production of cars in Poland amounts to some 15,000.

Syrena, 1960

IKA "Bergantin," 1960

After an unsuccessful attempt to set up her own industry with the *Justicialistica* make, Argentina has attracted investment by the USA and European automobile industries. Various special models are made, including the *IKA* (Industrias Kaiser Argentina) "Bergantin" which has a slightly altered *Alfa Romeo* "1900" body fitted with a "Jeep" engine.

The *Hong-Chi* was first seen in Europe at the 1960 Leipzig Fair. With a V-8 motor (100×90 mm, 5650 cc; $4'' \times 3\frac{5}{8}''$, 345 cu.in.) and automatic transmission the chassis and body follow earlier US designs. 紅旗

A domestic car industry was established in the Chinese People's Republic in 1955, with Russian technical aid. Since then production has become more independent, and comprises the *Hong-Chi* and *Dong-Feng* in unknown quanties.

Hong-Chi
(Red Flag), 1961

The Swedish car industry has its roots in venerable traditions, a wide experience of high-quality metalwork, and a discriminating home market. Before 1939 Swedish automobiles were practically unknown abroad, and even at home were not widely sold. After 1945 exports started in a small way, but it was not long before the modern Swedish makes were known the world over. They reflect partly the climatic and road conditions of their country of origin and partly an unprejudiced neutrality in design matters. Ideas are borrowed from both Europe and the USA, and quite a few components come from foreign firms. Nevertheless, the fundamental concept is Swedish—strength with good manners— and these qualities have proved so acceptable, both at home and abroad, that annual production was quadrupled in five years. It is now over 130,000 units a year, and can be expected to increase further.

Late in the 1880s a master painter, *Jöns Cederholm,* designed a steam carriage which was built in 1890-92 by his brother *Anders,* a master blacksmith. It had a single-cyl. (120 × 160 mm; $4\frac{3}{4}'' \times 6\frac{1}{4}''$) steam engine and reached a speed of about 9 mph, but proved impossible to steer since the back axle had no differential. The next twin-cyl. model (which is still in existence) was greatly improved, and had a clutch mechanism to overcome the differential problem. However, a number of test runs brought fresh difficulties to light, and the Cederholm brothers abandoned any further attempts.

Cederholm
1894

(Kloster Museum, Ystad)

Gustaf Erikson (1859-1922) joined the *Vagnfabrik AB i Södertälje* (Vabis) in 1897, where he built a motor carriage fitted with a water cooled 2-cyl. two-cycle engine; the ignition featured a spark plug of fireproof clay which had to be heated with a blowtorch before starting. An improved version was made shortly after, and is now in the Stockholm Technical Museum. Production became quite considerable after *Vabis* joined forces with *Scania* in 1911.

Erikson
1897/98

Sweden

The Svenska Aeroplan A. B. was founded in 1937 with government aid to build planes for the Swedish Air Force. Immediately after 1945 aircraft production lagged, and SAAB took over a project launched around 1939 for making a car based on the *DKW*. SAAB revised the original plans, and their first car, the "Model 92" which appeared in 1949, was a successful development of the DKW clearly incorporating their experience in aeronautical engineering. In 1955 SAAB changed from twin- to 3-cyl. motors. Driven by Erik Carlsson, a SAAB won the RAC Rally in 1960, 1961, and 1962, and the Monte Carlo Rallies in 1962 and 1963.

SAAB "92," 1950

The transverse 2-cyl. (80 × 76 mm, 764 cc; 3 ⅛" × 3", 46.7 cu.in.) engine was not greatly different from the DKW's. The car also had front-wheel drive, although the transmission design was entirely original. Modest weight and a carefully shaped body made for especially good running economy.

SAAB "93," 1956

A 3-cyl. (66 × 72.9 mm, 748 cc; 2⅝" × 2⅞", 45.6 cu.in.) motor raised the power from 25 to 38 bhp, and revised front suspension gave even better roadholding. This model won rallies all over the world, and was succeeded by the more powerful "93B," "93F," and "750 GT." The "95" with an 841 cc (50.1 cu.in.) engine and the "96," introduced in 1961, had further mechanical and body improvements.

SAAB "96," 1962

Volvo "P4," 1927

4-cyl. 75 × 110 mm, 1940 cc (3" × 4⅜", 118.5 cu.in.) with body after a design by the artist *Mas-Olle*

The *Volvo* (Latin for "I roll" or "I rotate") was a combined effort, organized by *Assar Gabrielson,* by a number of leading industrial concerns, including *Svenska Kugellagerfabriken, Pentaverken, Köpings Mekaniska Verkstad, Bofors,* and others. After a relatively modest start the firm developed substantially during the 1930s, gradually taking over a number of component suppliers. Their car production was accompanied by a growing output of trucks. Various experiments were made with hydraulic transmission, streamlined bodywork, etc., and inspiration seemed to come predominantly from the USA. A prototype of the "PV 444" appeared in 1944, and formed the starting point for the firm's success in the world market.

Volvo "PV 53-56," 1939

Swedish version of a medium-sized
US automobile.

Volvo "PV 444," 1947

4-cyl. 75×80 mm, 1414 cc (3″×3⅛″, 87 cu. in.).
This happy combination of European and American ideas in an entirely Swedish design laid the
foundations for Volvo's export of cars.

"PV 544," 1960-62

Introduced in 1958 and supplied in
single-carburetor (66 bhp) or twin-
carburetor (85 bhp) form; termed the
"PV 544S" in the latter case.

"P 1900," 1954

The first sports Volvo, differing from the other
post-1945 models in having a chassis under the
fiberglass reinforced plastic body. Only a few
were made, and production ceased in 1957.

Volvo "PV60," 1944

6-cyl. L-head, 3600 cc (220 cu. in.), the last
model with a wholly transatlantic look, giving no indication of the export successes to
come.

"122S Amazon," 1962

This model was brought out in 1957 with the
new B16A engine (79.37×80 mm, 1587 cc;
3⅛″×3⅛″, 96.7 cu. in.), developing 60 bhp,
and also fitted in the PV544. The sports
version with twin carburetors gave 85 bhp.

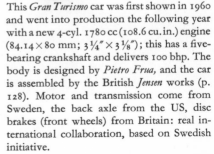

"P 1800," 1961

This *Gran Turismo* car was first shown in 1960
and went into production the following year
with a new 4-cyl. 1780 cc (108.6 cu. in.) engine
(84.14×80 mm; 3¼″×3⅛″); this has a five-
bearing crankshaft and delivers 100 bhp. The
body is designed by *Pietro Frua,* and the car
is assembled by the British *Jensen* works (p.
128). Motor and transmission come from
Sweden, the back axle from the US, disc
brakes (front wheels) from Britain: real international collaboration, based on Swedish
initiative.

Sweden

Scania, 1902

Vabis, 1910
4-cyl. 80×100 mm, 2000 cc
(3⅛″×4″, 122 cu.in.)

Maskinfabriks Aktiebolaget Scania, of Malmö, series-produced cars and trucks from 1902-1911, when they amalgamated with Vabis (p. 171) to form *Scania-Vabis*. This combine in 1924 moved to Södertälje, where production was concentrated on trucks. It is still a thriving concern, producing world-renowned diesel engines, diesel-powered trucks, and special vehicles. A subsidiary has been set up in Brazil. The radiator badge is a stylized representation of a pedal hub from the bicycles originally made by Scania, and the factory is one of the oldest with a continuous history in the automobile industry. No resumption of car production is planned, but the firm acts as VW's importer in Sweden.

Scania-Vabis "Type III"
1919, 4-cyl. 100×160 mm,
5000 cc (4″×6¼″, 366 cu.in.)

Thulin, 1923
4-cyl. 64×110, 1420 cc
(2½″×4⅜″, 86.6 cu.in.)

Enoch Thulin began building aircraft and aero-engines in Landskrona in 1914; in 1919 *Thulinwerken AB* changed to car production, which continued until 1928.

The modern car industry of the Soviet Union began in 1927 with the Moscow-built *Nami* ; other factories were established during the 1930s with American technical assistance, and the Ford "A" made a come back as the *GAZ* "A" (Gorkovskii Avto Zavod). This factory's model "M-1" of 1935 was an accurate copy of the 1934 Ford. The industry was reorganized after 1945, and from 1950-60 the annual production of cars has risen from 65,000 to 149,000.

There was only a sporadic automotive industry in Czarist Russia and her Baltic provinces, but the *Russko-Baltuskii Waggon-nyi Zavod* was active in Riga from 1909-13.

Nami "1," 1927
2-cyl. 84×105 mm
1164 cc (3¼″×4⅛″, 71 cu.in.)
НАМИ-1

ВОЛГА

Volga, 1959

Moskvitch "401," 1951
cf. Opel "Kadett"
МОСКВИЧ

Tchaika, 1962
built in Gorki, 5530 cc (338 cu.in.)
V-8 engine

The *ZIL* (Zavod imeni Likatjova) is the Soviet VIP's car, previously the ZIS (S for Stalin).

ЧАИКА

Zaporozhetz, 1961 ЗАПОРОЖЕЧ
air-cooled rear engine

ЗИЛ-Ш

ZIL "111," 1960

Road conditions, climate, economic factors, enormous distances, and rigorous traffic laws have provided a background for the American automobile entirely different from the European, and, in spite of a widespread technical rapprochement, attitudes on the two sides of the Atlantic are basically different. This applies equally to the designer and the owner-driver. The moment the automobile became a technical reality, US manufacturers endeavored to produce cars which would give the driver as few problems as possible. Planetary gears were not fitted to early American cars as mechanical ingenuities but because of a realistic recognition of the average driver's inability to cope with the sliding pinions of a manual transmission.

In the USA the car became, from the very beginning, an everyday tool—neither a luxury on which rapacious treasury ministers could impose extortionate and discriminatory taxes, nor a field in which engineers and inventors with varying degrees of ability could perform their technical somersaults. Cars were first and foremost a subject for production engineers, provided that a practical model could be supplied at a reasonable price. It may well be that this unsentimental outlook has been more mature than the more artistic-technical traditions of Europe, though it comes hard to a European to embrace the idea of automobiles as consumer goods. Respect for an elegant solution to a technical problem is too ingrained, and in a continent which has done its level best to destroy itself in unproductive wars the car still retains a certain glamorous air of adventure. The atmosphere is quite different in a country which between 1900 and 1960 produced 185 million motorcars, and is producing them at a rate of 6-7 million every year.

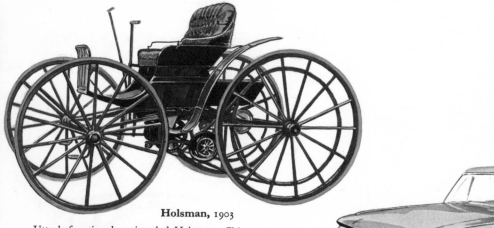

Holsman, 1903

Utterly functional motives led *Holsman,* a Chicago architect, to motorize the classic, horse-drawn "Highwheeler," which could cut its way down through the mud to firm ground. A twin-cyl. air-cooled engine (81 × 101.6 mm, 1050 cc; 3¼″ × 4″, 63.8 cu.in.) was fitted under the seat, with belt drive to the rear wheels. The entire motor could be moved to provide clutch-action through slackening the rope-drive. In production 1902-1909.

Rambler "Classic Super 6," 1962

The outcome of modern production techniques, present-day traffic conditions, and the same realistic approach as Holsman's "Highwheeler."

Rambler, 1904
2-cyl. (127 × 152.4 mm; 5″ × 6″) under front seat.
Thomas B. Jeffery, a cycle manufacturer, built the first Rambler in 1901; the make became the *Nash* in 1917, and in 1954 merged with Hudson to form *American Motors Corporation.* Hudson then disappeared, and Rambler became a separate make under the AMC.

Nash, 1946

Charles W. Nash
left General Motors in 1916, took over Rambler, and in 1936 joined forces with the *Kelvinator Corporation,* which made refrigerators.

Nash "Rambler," 1950
With commendable initiative Nash introduced a smaller model in 1950, and revived the make's original name. The size and Italian-styled body anticipated later trends.

A financier, *J. L. Hudson,* gave his name to the make established 1909 by *Roy D. Chapin* and *Howard E. Coffin.*

Hudson "Six-40," 1915

Hudson "Hornet," 1953
One of the last models (6-cyl. 5047 cc—306 cu.in.) before the merger with Nash. Hudson was discontinued after 1957.

Terraplane, 1933

Essex "Coach," 1922
4-cyl. 85.7 × 127 mm,
2860 cc   (3⅜″ × 5″, 178.9 cu. in.)
Hudson's cheaper, competitive model.

To recoup its losses between 1929-32 Hudson brought out the "Terraplane." For a while the same name was used for certain Essex models.

The developments which brought Nash and Hudson together (under the Nash-Kelvinator Corporation) serve to illustrate the fundamental importance of production and sales organization in the US car industry. Nash was a brilliant organizer, as was Chapin, with a knack for finding clever engineers. The link-up of Nash and Kelvinator was carried out in the interests of production. Hudson (which was failing fast as a make) was included in the concern in order to increase the productive potential. *George Wilcken Romney,* who came from Nash to manage American Motors, made masterly use of the doubtful possibilities by concentrating all production on the rather small "Rambler" model.

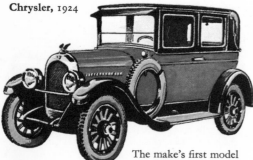

Nash-Healey, 1951
Healey "Silverstone"
chassis   3800 cc (231 cu. in.)
6-cyl. *Nash* engine

Chrysler, 1924

6-cyl.
76.2 × 114.3 mm
3100 cc (3″ × 4½″, 190.8 cu. in.)

The make's first model designed by *Fred. M. Zeder, Owen Shelton,* and *Carl Breer.*

Walter Percy Chrysler was a mechanic by training and inclination. After working with the American Locomotive Company he came to Buick in 1911 under Charles Nash, and later took over the management of the factory, but left General Motors in 1921. He then attempted to reorganize Willys Overland, before taking over Maxwell-Chalmers in 1921. On the basis of these activities, Chrysler launched his own make, a cautious technical advance.

Two new lines, Plymouth and De Soto, appeared in 1928 as separate makes. Also

in 1928 Dodge was added to the Chrysler line. The brothers *John F.* and *Horace E. Dodge* originally supplied chassis, motors, and transmissions to Ford, but broke with him and established their own make in 1914. The Chrysler-Dodge group became the third largest manufacturer in the USA, and between 1925-29 increased its annual output to around 400,000 units. The Depression brought a sharp setback, but the difficulties were overcome. The Chrysler Corporation now accounts for 12 per cent of annual US production, and has shown refreshing technical independence. De Soto was dropped in 1960.

The appearance of the Chrysler and De Soto "Airflows" was too unusual to sell well in 1934, and more traditional lines reappeared in 1938.

Chrysler "Airflow," 1934

Chrysler "Imperial," 1931

This 8-cyl. (88.8 × 127 mm, 6300 cc; 3½″ × 5″, 384.8 cu.in.) model was Chrysler's much-admired rival to the V-12 Lincoln and V-16 Cadillac of those days.

Chrysler "300 H," 1962
V-8 (106.2 × 95 mm, 6768 cc; 4⅛″ × 3¾″, 413 cu.in.)

Dodge, 1920
4-cyl.
(98.4 × 112.6 mm, 3400 cc; 3⅞″ × 4½″, 208 cu.in.)

De Soto, 1952

Named after the discoverer of the Mississippi River; Chrysler's medium-priced car 1929-60.

Plymouth, 1949
6-cyl. (82.55 × 111.1 mm, 3567 cc; 3¼″ × 4⅜″, 217.8 cu.in.) Chrysler's low-priced competitor with Ford and Chevrolet.

Checker, 1959

This make was first built for taxi work, but production of passenger cars was begun in 1958 (6-cyl. 84.13 × 111.1 mm, 3703 cc; 3¼″ × 4⅜″, 226.2 cu.in.)

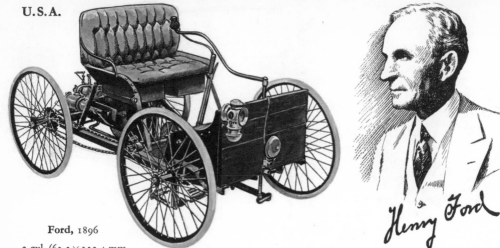

Ford, 1896
2-cyl. (63.5 × 152.4 mm,
970 cc; 2½″ × 6″, 59 cu. in.) experimental model.

Henry Ford (1863-1947) made a greater contribution than any other designer to the widespread use of the automobile. His Model "T" formed the background for the impressive network of highways in America. Ford's first experimental model was sold, but was later bought back and now stands in a showcase in the Henry Ford Museum, Dearborn, Michigan. In its hand-made details it betrays self-willed design concepts, although it bears the mark of influence by Pennington's more unrestrained ideas (p. 197).

It is a strange fact that the man who laid the foundations for such far-reaching technological progress came into the world by candle light—for electric light had not been invented at that time—and died in the same candle-light—the city's electricity had failed.

Ford "T," 1908/09
4-cyl. (95.2 × 101.6 mm, 2900 cc;
3¾″ × 4″, 176.7 cu. in.)

A ignition switch E combined brake and clutch lever
B carburetor control F gearshift pedal (forward—2 gears)
C hand throttle G reverse pedal
D ignition adjustment H foot brake

Ford "T coupé," 1924
Simple design, good materials, and standardized parts were the recipe for 15 million Model "T"s sold at steadily decreasing prices 1908-27.

The imperishable Model "T" became a victim of its own legendary ability to cope with anything. As roads were developed in the United States, cars became more sophisticated than the "T," and a new Ford was needed to meet the competition. In December 1927 the Model "A" was announced.

Ford "A," 1928

4-cyl. 98.4×108 mm, 3285 cc
(3⅞″×4¼″, 200.5 cu.in.)

Ford "V-8," 1932
77.8×95.25 mm, 3622 cc (3″×3¾″, 221 cu.in.)

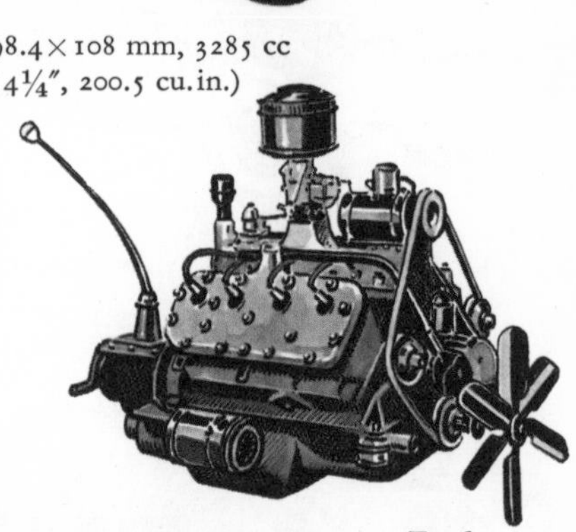

Ford V-8 motor, 1932

Even before the sales graph for the Model "T" began to drop off, Ford was already working on possible successors. His son, *Edsel,* wanted to use a 6-cyl. motor, but since his failture with the 6-cyl. Model "K" in 1906 Henry Ford had the deepest mistrust for units with that number of cylinders. From 1922-25 he made exhaustive experiments with an X-8 air-cooled engine; the design was, however, too ingenious, and the Model "A" was designed as a desperate though successful stop-gap model. Henry Ford's real masterpiece as a production leader was the V-8, introduced in 1932 as an answer to Chevrolet's 6-cyl. motor of 1929. It was first fitted to the Model "B," which was a revised Model "A." The V-8 motor represented a triumph of metal-casting technique of considerable consequence. The first 6-cyl. Ford only appeared in 1940.

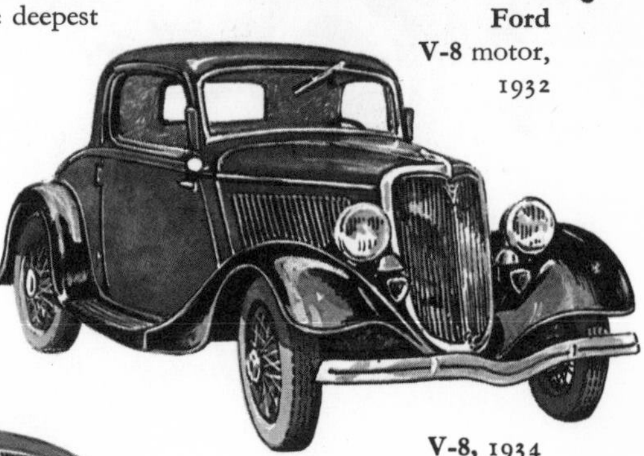

V-8, 1934

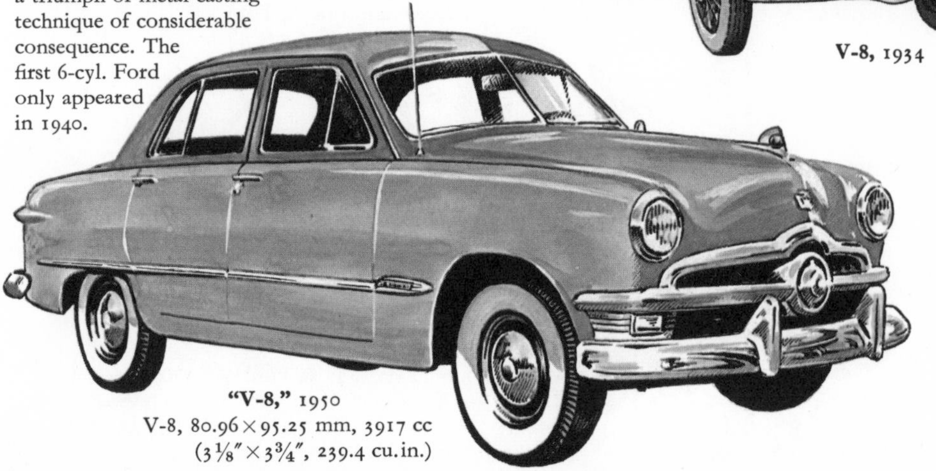

"V-8," 1950
V-8, 80.96×95.25 mm, 3917 cc
(3⅛″×3¾″, 239.4 cu.in.)

Mercury "V-8," 1939
$(81 \times 95.25$ mm, 3917 cc; $3\frac{1}{8}'' \times 3\frac{3}{4}''$, 239.4 cu. in.)
Medium price range model, 1939,
made by *Lincoln*.

Falcon, 1960
6-cyl. 88.9×63.5 mm, 2364 cc
$(3\frac{1}{2}'' \times 2\frac{1}{2}''$, 144 cu. in.)

Edsel, 1958
(V-8, 101.6×88.9 mm, 5920 cc; $4'' \times 3\frac{1}{2}''$, 361
cu. in.). Announced in 1957 as a new make;
production ceased in 1959.

It is to Edsel Ford's credit that Ford acquired *H. M. Leland*'s failing *Lincoln* factory, and continued the make as Ford's elite line (named after Abraham Lincoln, whom Leland greatly admired). Edsel Ford produced a superb car, and it is bitterly ironical that the make named after him was a fiasco, which cost the Ford Motor Co. 250 million dollars.

Lincoln "L," 1931, the last of the old-type Lincoln V-8's.

Lincoln "Zephyr,"
1939
V-12, 70×95 mm, 4378 cc
$(2\frac{3}{4}'' \times 3\frac{3}{4}''$, 266 cu. in.)
a development of the Ford V-8.

Lincoln "Continental," 1962
V-8, 109.2×94 mm, 7046 cc $(4\frac{3}{8}'' \times 3\frac{3}{4}''$, 430 cu. in.)
Ford Motor Co.'s prestige model.

From 1940-48 Edsel Ford had a "Continental" built in limited numbers. The idea was revived in 1955 with a "Mark II" version, which has since been much refined both aesthetically and mechanically.

Buick, 1912

General Motors was formed on September 16, 1908, and after the first few stormy years the combine consolidated itself as the world's largest producer of cars. No. 75,000,000 came off the concern's US assembly line in 1962. Passenger cars form over 75 per cent of GM's output.

David Dunbar Buick abandoned the manufacture of plumbing supplies in favor of motor manufacture in 1902, and produced 6 cars during 1903. *W. V. Durant* took over the business in 1904 as the foundation stone for GM. D. D. Buick was one of the first in the USA to use valve-in-head motors.

Buick, 1926
6-cyl. 76.2 × 120.7 mm, 3500 cc
(3″ × 4¾″, 201 cu.in.)
a sturdy, valve-in-head design.

Buick "Super," 1950

From 1931 Buick had 8-in-line motors, until V-8 motors were introduced in 1953.

Buick "Special," 1962

Besides two V-8 motors, cast in aluminum and iron respectively, Buick put a cast-iron V-6 engine on the market in the latter part of 1961 (92.2 × 81.3 mm, 3720 cc; 3⅝″ × 3⅛″, 227 cu.in.; 135 bhp).

Cadillac "V-16," 1930,
7400 cc (450 cu. in.)

Cadillac "B," 1904
1-cyl. 127 × 127 mm,
1620 cc (5″ × 5″, 98.9 cu. in.)

Henry Martin Leland was a skilled engineer, whose firm came into the motor industry from machine tools and marine engines when Ford left the *Detroit Automobile Co.* founded in 1900. This company changed its name to *Cadillac Automobile Co,* in 1902.

Cadillac joined GM in 1909, but remained under Leland's management until 1917. Its technical qualities were confirmed by the award, in 1908, of the British *Dewar Trophy* for achievement in automobile engineering in proving standardization of parts. Three cars were dismantled, the parts mixed up—and three roadworthy cars were assembled from the pieces. The make won the Dewar Trophy again in 1913 with its electric self-starter, which was a standard fitting from 1912.

V-8, 96.8 × 92 mm,
5424 cc (3⅞″ × 3⅝″,
331 cu. in.) 210 bhp—
despite the name,
no sports car.

Cadillac "Le Mans," 1953

Care in assembly and a fastidious selection of materials won the Cadillac its reputation, and the V-8 model introduced for 1915 was kept practically unchanged until 1927. Then followed the legendary V-16 designed by *Charles F. Kettering* (1876-1958)—inventor of the self-starter—who led GM's research department for many years and designed, among other things, the synchromesh transmission. Kettering's later research work on high-compression motors sparked the development of US car engines after 1949, and his lively mind explored all fields.

Cadillac "75," Coupé de Ville, 1962
V-8, 101.6 × 98.4 mm, 6392 cc
(4″ × 3⅞″, 390 cu. in.) 325 bhp

General Motors' prestige make was named after the French explorer Antoine Laumet de la Mothe Cadillac.

The *La Salle,* introduced by the factory in 1921, was named the same way; but the idea of a cheap Cadillac was dropped after 1940.

Chevrolet, 1911

The Swiss immigrant racing driver *Louis-Joseph Chevrolet* designed the car which paved the way for the marque.

The popular "Royal Mail" gave way to the 4-cyl. "490," which was the main model from 1916-23.

"Royal Mail," 1914

Chevrolet "V-8," 1918
At the time of the make's takeover by GM a V-8 engine was fitted, but it never gained the popularity of the "490."

"Coppercooled"
4-cyl. 88.9×88.9 mm
2200 cc (3 ½" × 3 ½",
134.7 cu.in.) air-cooled

1923
abandoned the same year

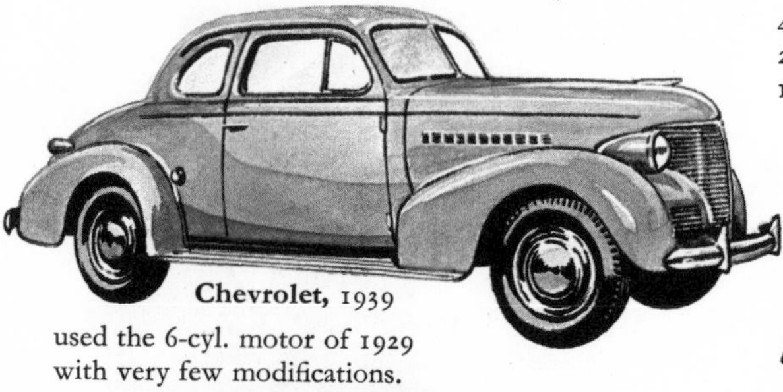

Chevrolet, 1939
used the 6-cyl. motor of 1929 with very few modifications.

Chevrolet, 1925

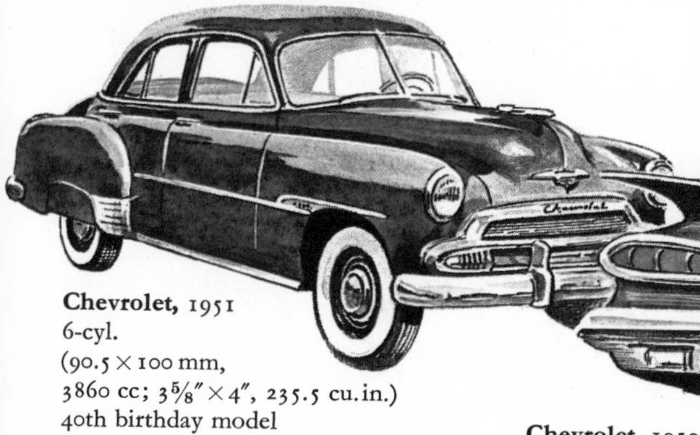

Chevrolet, 1951
6-cyl.
(90.5 × 100 mm,
3860 cc; 3⅝" × 4", 235.5 cu.in.)
40th birthday model

1959

Chevrolet, 1959

U.S.A.

Chevrolet "Corvette," 1953
The make's first attempt at a sports car

The "Corvette" was brought out with the perennial 6-cyl. Chevrolet motor in a slightly modified form and a fiberglass reinforced plastic body. Later the model was given V-8 power and underwent drastic changes.

"Corvair," 1960

"Chevy II," 1961
A new model, midway between the large cars and the "Corvair." 4-cyl. 98.4×82.55 mm, 2509 cc (3⅛″×3¼″, 153 cu.in.) 6-cyl. 90.5×82.55 mm, 3200cc (3⅝″×3¼″, 194 cu.in.)

The "Corvair" was Chevrolet's first "compact" model, with a refreshingly different specification: all-independent suspension, and an air-cooled motor at the rear—atoning for the unsuccessful "Coppercooled" 26 years earlier.

1-cyl.
114.3×152.4 mm
1563 cc (4½″×6″,
Ransom Eli Olds' renowned "curved-dash" was America's first popular car.

Oldsmobile, 1901
95.4 cu.in.)

Oldsmobile, 1929
R. E. Olds left the factory in 1904 and founded *Reo*. The Oldsmobile then became one of the first makes in GM, and in the 1920s was a typical US medium-priced car. The first V-8 appeared in 1916.

Oldsmobile "Limited,"
1911
The old song "In my merry Oldsmobile" had nothing to do with the older cars, but was launched at a dealers' convention in San Francisco when the magnificent "Limited" was announced. A huge 6-cyl. motor (127×152.4 mm, 11,600 cc; 5″×6″, 707 cu.in.) lay under the impressive bonnet, and this colossal car was shod with 43×5 tires—the largest ever on any US car.

Oldsmobile "Super 88," 1961   V-8, 104.8 × 93.7 mm, 6458 cc (4⅛" × 3¾", 394 cu.in).

Oakland "24," 1910

originally produced by the *Oakland Motor Car Co.,* joined GM in 1909, ceased in 1932

Pontiac, 1926

6-cyl. medium-price car, rubber-mounted engine, introduced to supplement the Oakland, which it later replaced.

Pontiac "Tempest," 1962

In the enormous General Motors organization the individual "Divisions" (i.e. makes) have a certain amount of autonomy, although they work in close collaboration within the over-all framework. For example, the same body pressings are used over a wide range of different models and makes. Mechanical features also recur from make to make, and the production pattern forms a gigantic jigsaw puzzle with innumerable components which can be assembled in varying combinations so as to cater to every price bracket in the market.

This "compact" model was announced in 1961 with a 4-cyl. or V-8 engine, a gearbox in unit with the back axle, and a curved, flexible drive shaft linking the motor and transmission.

La Salle, 1939

Make founded in 1927 as a medium-price *Cadillac*; V-8 engine.

Studebaker "C," 1904. This firm began in 1852 as carriage-builders, introduced electric cars in 1902, and gasoline automobiles in 1904.

"Commander V-8,"
1951

Loewy's daring body design for the 1947 Studebaker changed little until 1953. The V-8 motor came in 1951.

Studebaker "Lark," 1962
6-cyl. 76.2 × 101.6 mm, 2779 cc
(3″ × 4″, 169.4 cu.in.)
V-8 90.5 × 82.55 mm, 4248 cc (3⅝″ × 3¼″, 289 cu.in.) and a larger V-8.

Packard, 1930

James Ward Packard's first car was built in 1899 through pique at a mediocre car he had bought.

Packard, 1906

4-cyl. 114.3 × 139.7 mm, 5730 cc (4½″ × 5½″, 349.9 cu.in.)

With his brother William, J. W. Packard ran a factory making electric cables and the like. When the first car was built the *Ohio Automobile Co.* was formed, with both capital and technical know-how supplied by *Henry Bourne Joy*. The *Packard Motor Car Co.* was registered in Detroit in 1903, and after good 4-, 6-, and 8-cyl. models produced an impressive V-12 in 1915. The dwindling quality market caused Packard to merge with Studebaker in 1954. The make disappeared altogether in 1959.

"Clipper Super," 1955
8-cyl. 88.9 × 108 mm, 5360 cc
(3½″ × 4¼″, 327 cu.in.)
One of the last independent Packards.

The numerous vanished makes of the USA represent all shades of the automobile industry: mechanical nine-day wonders, highly imaginative designs, dream cars with no hope of a future, the merely boring and mediocre, and the inevitable progressive ideas doomed to failure: sometimes because their creator was ahead of his time, sometimes because capital and the other essential production facilities were lacking. In some cases the technological qualities were dubious, but more often the reason for a make's disappearance is to be found in inadequate production and marketing organization.

In 1894 the brothers *Edgar* and *Elmer Apperson* completed a car which had been begun by *Elwood Haynes* three years earlier. The partnership soon broke up, and the Haynes make survived until 1924. The Apperson went into liquidation two years later.

Apperson, 1916
6-cyl. 88.9 × 130.2 mm,
4850 cc (3 ½″ × 5 ⅛″, 296 cu. in.)

Arnolt-Bristol
1953
US initiative
British chassis (see p. 120)
Italian body (Bertone)

Auburn,
1932,
12-cyl.

AU·932

Part of the *Cord* group from 1924

Baker "Runabout," 1901

A well-designed light electric car for town use, typical of its period.

Bantam, 1938

The American Austin Co.'s *Austin* 7, called *Bantam* from 1930.

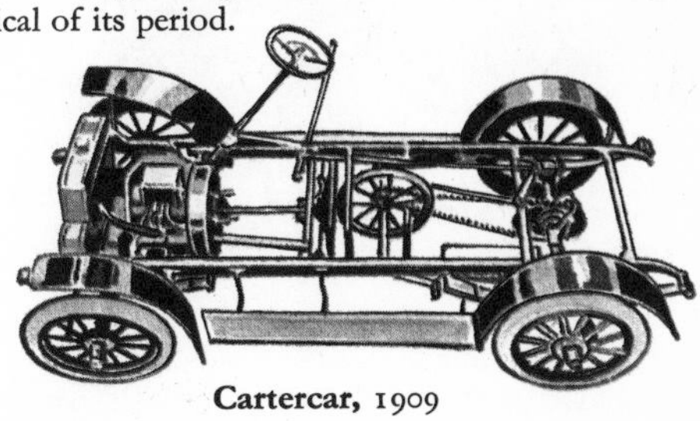

Cartercar, 1909

A patent friction drive induced *W. C. Durant* to incorporate this make in General Motors.

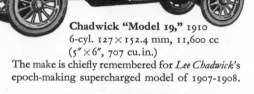

Chadwick "Model 19," 1910
6-cyl. 127×152.4 mm, 11,600 cc
(5″×6″, 707 cu.in.)
The make is chiefly remembered for *Lee Chadwick*'s
epoch-making supercharged model of 1907-1908.

Cord "810," 1936

Gordon Buehrig's Cord bodywork was so revolutionary that it was patented on May 17, 1934.

Errett Lobban Cord wrote one of the more colorful chapters in American motoring history when he built up, during the Depression years, a concern embracing *Auburn, Duesenberg, Lycoming Motors,* etc. which launched, in 1929, a new make named after the president of the *Cord Corporation*. The Cord make was not just a rehash of well-known components, but an unusual car with front-wheel drive built under the patents of racing designer *Harry Armenius Miller,* who in 1924 revived the De Dion axle (though using it for the front wheels). The Cord "L-29" was produced until the end of 1932, and was replaced by the "810" presented in New York in 1935. Production snags and teething troubles with the unorthodox design spoiled the undoubted sales potential, and production ceased in 1937.

Christie, 1909

Walter Christie produced some peculiar racing models, including one with two transverse-mounted motors and four-wheel drive. His 1909 taxicab anticipated the layout of the BMC "Mini" (p. 130).

Hugh Chalmers, vice-president of the National Cash Register Co., was a founder member, in a sales capacity, of the *Chalmers Detroit* make. The *Chalmers Motor Co.* was formed in 1911. It joined forces with Maxwell in 1917 and was taken over by W. P. Chrysler in 1923.

Chalmers, 1911

Columbia "Victoria,"
1901

The *Electric Vehicle Co.* intended to monopolize automobile production and taxi operation in the USA with such cars. Two battery-powered electric motors were mounted on the rear axle.

V-8, 89×95 mm, 4700 cc
(3½″×3¾″, 289 cu.in.)
Lycoming engine with centrifugal
blower and electrically preselected
vacuum-operated gearshift.

Cord "812," 1937

Cord "L-29," 1929-32
8-cyl. 82.55×114.3 mm, 4934 cc
(3¼″×4½″, 299 cu.in.)
Front-wheel drive with De Dion layout
and inboard drum brakes.

Crosley, 1946

In 1939 *Powell Crosley Jr.* launched a twin-cyl.
car, which in 1946 was given a 4-cyl. single
o.h.c. engine (63.5×57.14 mm, 721 cc;
2½″×2¼″, 44 cu.
in.). For a time the
Siata (p. 164) used
this engine.

Cunningham was the name of three quite independent makes; a steam-car of 1901, a
quality car made by· *Jas. Cunningham, Son &
Co.* of Rochester N. Y., and finally those
built by *Briggs S. Cunningham* during the
years 1951-55, although these hardly deserve
the term "series-produced." The first of these
three left no trace; the second was justifiably
known as the "American Rolls-Royce"; the
third was a praiseworthy effort to produce an
American automobile able to compete with
the world's leading sports cars. The Rochester
factory began making cars in 1909, took up
regular production in 1911, and from 1916
sold a magnificent V-8 with a superb standard of finish. Automobiles were abandoned
in 1936 when the firm changed over to
electrical goods.

Cunningham
1919
(Rochester)

V-8, 95.25×127 mm,
7250 cc (3¾″×5″, 442
cu.in.)

191

Cunningham "C-4R"
1952

This well-built car (Chrysler V-8 motor, tubular chassis, coil springs, De Dion back axle, and 5-speed transmission) won Cunningham a 4th place and a class win at Le Mans.

Briggs S. Cunningham forsook his real love, sailing, in 1950, to create a car able to hold its own in international competition. After an experimental entry at Le Mans in 1950 with two Cadillacs he made the first *Cunningham* (V-8 Chrysler) in 1951, and the marque gained an over-all 3rd place in 1953 and 1954. The last model (in 1955) had an *Offenhauser* engine.

Cunningham, 1953
Chrysler motor, *Vignale* bodywork

Doble "E-24," 1930

Abner Doble built his first steam-car in 1906, and began production proper in 1914. His costly, precision-made cars were technically outstanding and majestic in appearance.

8-cyl. 95 × 121 mm, 6882 cc (3¾″ × 4¾″, 420 cu.in) twin o.h. camshafts, four valves per cylinder, centrifugal blower—and a price to match.

Duesenberg "SJ," 1933

Frederick Samuel Duesenberg and his brother *August* came to the USA from Germany during their youth, and grew up in the first flourishing years of the automobile. Fred's first design was the *Mason* (1904-1909), which became the *Maytag* in 1910. In 1913 the *Duesenberg Motor Co.* was formed, mainly to build engines, and the first car bearing the Duesenberg name, the Model "A," appeared in 1920 with an 8-cyl. motor bearing unmistakable signs of its racing background. A Duesenberg won the French Grand Prix in 1921. In 1928 the magnificent "J" appeared, to be joined in 1932 by the "SJ" supercharged version. Production ceased in 1937.

8-cyl.
85.7 × 114.3 mm, **Du Pont "G,"** 1929
5277 cc ($3\frac{3}{8}'' \times 4\frac{1}{2}''$, 322 cu. in.)
Produced 1920-32

The *Franklin* was another un-orthodox US make, fitted between 1902-34 with air-cooled motors with 4, 6, and 12 cylinders. *Herbert H. Franklin* left his publishing business to become an automobile producer when he discovered a number of unused patents for a special casting technique.

Duryea "Surrey," 1904

Charles E. Duryea's firm (p. 16) had subsidiaries in Belgium and Britain, where this 3-cyl. model was built.

Elmore, 1904

A make taken over by General Motors in 1909 for the sake of its two-cycle engine.

EMF "A-30," 1910

A make, which joined *Studebaker*, founded by *B. F. Everitt,* *W. E. Metzger,* and *W. E. Flanders*

Franklin, 1905
4-cyl. 72.55 × 72.55 mm,
1200 cc ($2\frac{7}{8}'' \times 2\frac{7}{8}''$, 73 cu. in.)

Air-cooled motor mounted transversely under the hood, with exhaust pipe pointing to the front.

Franklin "145,"
1930
6-cyl. 88.9 × 120.7 mm, 4490 cc ($3\frac{1}{2}'' \times 4\frac{3}{4}''$, 274 cu. in.) air-cooled, with squirrel-cage blower.

Kaiser, 1951   **Frazer,** 1947

In 1943 the industrial magnate Henry J. Kaiser, who built "Liberty Ships" during the war years, made it known that he was going to enter the automobile industry when the war was over. Three months after this *Joseph W. Frazer* retired as president of *Willys-Overland*. On July 26, 1945 the connection between these two events was confirmed by the formation of the *Kaiser-Frazer Corporation,* which announced its new line in January 1946 and began series-production a few months later. Frazer had worked in the car industry all his life (with GM, Pierce-Arrow, and others) and with him the *Graham-Paige Corporation* entered the new combine, which did not produce technically outstanding cars. In 1953 the Kaiser-Frazer Corporation merged with *Willys-Overland,* and when production of Kaiser and Frazer creased in the US these makes continued to be made in assembly plants in South America, *Industrias Kaiser Argentina* and *Willys-Overland do Brasil.*

Sears AllState, 1952

K-F's small car, the "Henry J," fitted with a 2190 cc (134 cu.in.) Willys engine, was handled in 1952 by the *Sears, Roebuck & Co.,* and was listed in their mail order catalogue. A car was marketed in the same way by this company around 1910.

Sears "M," 1909

The Sears, Roebuck & Co. mail order catalogue of 1909-12 stated encouragingly that "mechanical skill is unnecessary with a Sears car; the instruction book will make everything clear in half-an-hour." A twin-cylinder model, built in Sear's own factory.

Graham, 1938

Paige-Detroit, 1909

3-cyl. 95.25 × 101.6 mm, 2170 cc (3¾″ × 4″, 132.6 cu.in.) 2-cycle engine. *H. M. Jewett* was the engineer behind *Fred Paige* (who was in insurance). The make was taken over by the brothers *Joseph, Robert,* and *Ray Graham* in 1928, and renamed the Graham-Paige; it later became part of Kaiser-Frazer.

6 cyl. 82 × 111 mm, 3500 cc (3¼″ × 4⅜″, 217.8 cu.in.), centrifugal blower. The make's sporting character led to the British *Lammas-Graham,* a supercharged Graham chassis with English-style custom bodywork, in 1937, and a 5250 cc (321 cu.in.) Graham won the last race run at Brooklands (August 7, 1939).

Hupmobile, 1913
4-cyl. 82.55 × 85.73 mm, 1840 cc
(3¼″ × 3⅜″, 112 cu.in.)

Charles D. Hastings was the organizer and *Robert C. Hupp* the engineer for Hupmobile, which came on the market in 1908. Hupp left in 1911.

Hupmobile, 1931
6-cyl. 82.55 × 108 mm, 3550 cc (3¼″ × 4¼″, 211.5 cu.in.)

Hastings brought the make through the depression years of 1920-21, and his successor *Dubois Young* expanded the firm in 1928 by acquiring *Chandler-Cleveland.* In 1938 Hupmobile took over Cord's body dies, but car production ceased in 1941 and the make did not reappear after the war.

International Harvester,
1910
4-cyl. 95.25 × 95.25 mm, 2725 cc (3¾″ × 3¾″, 166 cu.in.) o.h.v., air-cooled. Made 1907-13 by the famous agricultural implements firm, for use in muddy conditions.

Kiblinger, 1907
2-cyl. air-cooled flat-twin motor.

Kissel, 1921

William L. Kissel and his brothers originally made farm machinery, although the cars they made from 1908-30 were far from agricultural in character. The "Gold Bug" speedster appeared in 1918 with six cylinders (8-cyl. from 1927).

Locomobile, 1899

A 2-cyl. steam-car, built by the *Locomobile Company of America,* which was founded in that year and took over the *Stanley* twins' first design. In 1902 the company changed to gasoline automobiles under the technical management of *Andrew L. Riker.*

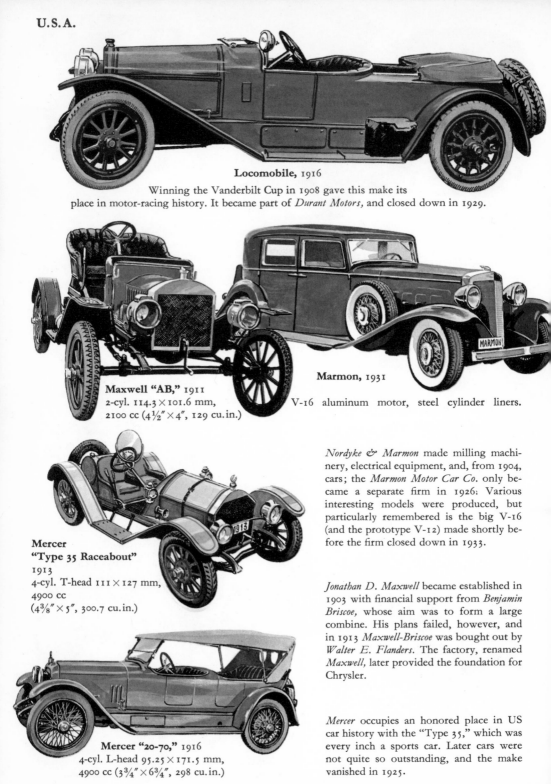

Locomobile, 1916

Winning the Vanderbilt Cup in 1908 gave this make its
place in motor-racing history. It became part of *Durant Motors,* and closed down in 1929.

Maxwell "AB," 1911
2-cyl. 114.3 × 101.6 mm,
2100 cc (4½″ × 4″, 129 cu. in.)

Marmon, 1931

V-16 aluminum motor, steel cylinder liners.

**Mercer
"Type 35 Raceabout"**
1913
4-cyl. T-head 111 × 127 mm,
4900 cc
(4⅜″ × 5″, 300.7 cu. in.)

Mercer "20-70," 1916
4-cyl. L-head 95.25 × 171.5 mm,
4900 cc (3¾″ × 6¾″, 298 cu. in.)

Nordyke & Marmon made milling machinery, electrical equipment, and, from 1904,
cars; the *Marmon Motor Car Co.* only became a separate firm in 1926: Various
interesting models were produced, but
particularly remembered is the big V-16
(and the prototype V-12) made shortly before the firm closed down in 1933.

Jonathan D. Maxwell became established in
1903 with financial support from *Benjamin
Briscoe,* whose aim was to form a large
combine. His plans failed, however, and
in 1913 *Maxwell-Briscoe* was bought out by
Walter E. Flanders. The factory, renamed
Maxwell, later provided the foundation for
Chrysler.

Mercer occupies an honored place in US
car history with the "Type 35," which was
every inch a sports car. Later cars were
not quite so outstanding, and the make
vanished in 1925.

8-cyl. 58.8×89 mm, 2000 cc
(2⅜″×3½″, 122 cu.in.)
This classic racing car was a
triumph of engine design.

Miller, 1923

Harry Armenius Miller (1875-1943) was a
brilliant engine designer. Influenced by the
early work of Ernest Henry and Ettore
Bugatti, he developed splendid motors
which still today dominate the American
racing scene under the Offenhauser name.
His inspiring designs later persuaded Bugatti to adopt twin o.h. camshafts.

Owen Magnetic,
1917-18

The *Owen Magnetic* was
made for a short time by
Baker, Rauch & Lang Co.
A 6-cyl. engine powered
a dynamo which supplied
current to an electric motor driving the back
wheels, to achieve gear-
less transmission.
Colonel Pope (p. 18) came
out in 1903 with the Pope-
Toledo, Pope-Hartford, Pope-
Waverly, and Pope-Tribune.

**Pennington
Autocar,** 1896
2-cyl. 62.5×305 mm,
1868 cc (2½″×12″, 114 cu.in.)

Edward Joel Pennington blandly announced in 1895
that he had solved all the problems of motor design with an engine having neither carburetor nor
radiator. The cylinders were steel tubes, and long
enough to "cool themselves." Henry Ford fell for
the idea when making his first experimental model.
So did H. J. Lawson, who founded the British
"Great Horseless Carriage Co."; he, however,
paid $500,000 for the Pennington patents.
Pennington died in 1911.

Pope-Toledo "VII," 1906

Pierce "Arrow," 1904
2-cyl. 100×120.65 mm, 1760 cc
(4″×4¾″, 105.6 cu.in.)

George N. Pierce, after making birdcages and refrigerators, became a bicycle manufacturer, and sold his first car in 1901. Pierce-Arrow was bought out by Studebaker in 1928, but regained its independence in 1933. It closed down in 1938, but not before it had produced an admirable 12-cyl. model.

Pierce-Arrow "A," 1930
8-cyl. 88.9×127 mm, 6300 cc
(3½″×5″, 385 cu.in.)

Reo, 1904

This single-cylinder automobile was launched by *Ransom E. Olds* (whose initials it carried) when he left Oldsmobile in 1904. Reo made passenger cars until 1936.

Ruxton, 1930
8-cyl. front-
wheel drive

The Ruxton was produced by *New Era Motors,* which absorbed *Moon, Gardner,* and *Kissel.*

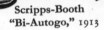

**Scripps-Booth
"Bi-Autogo," 1913**

Scripps Booth
experimental model, 1913

James Scripps Booth was a highly original designer though much of his effort never passed the experimental model stage. A little cyclecar (*left*) was European-inspired, while his monstrous cross between a car and a motorcycle was quite extraordinary—and next to impossible to steer. The make was taken over in 1916 by GM, who gave it a more normal character before it disappeared in 1921.

The twin brothers *Francis E. and Freelan O. Stanley* first applied their talents to making violins and photographic plates. They took over the rights for *George D. Whitney*'s steam-car in 1896, altered the design, then sold out to their partners *J. B. Walker* and *A. L. Barber*. The latter soon split up, each starting his own factory; Walker's *Mobile* was in existence 1899-1903, Barber's *Locomobile* (pp. 195-96) was dropped in favor of gasoline cars after 1903. The Stanley brothers bought the Locomobile steam-car interests in 1901 and in 1906 a Stanley steam-car set a land speed record of 127:66 mph, and in a 1907 record attempt a Stanley car reached 197 mph before crashing.

Stutz "Bearcat," 1917

4-cyl. 101.6×152.4 mm, 5990 cc (4″×6″, 301.6 cu.in.) 16 side-valves. *H. C. Stutz* left the firm soon afterward.

Stutz "DV 32," 1931

8-cyl. 85×114 mm, 5277 cc (3⅜″×4½″, 358 cu.in.) twin o.h.c., 32 valves

Harry C. Stutz was one of the USA's most prolific designers. He began with the *American Underslung* in 1905, and in 1911 the first *Stutz* finished 11th at Indianapolis. A whole series of high-quality sports cars followed. In 1919 Stutz left the firm to found HCS, which failed in 1924. Stutz ceased production in 1935.

Stoddard-Dayton, 1911

4-cyl. 5150 cc (314 cu.in.). This was one of the first US makes which offered models with Knight sleeve-valves. Absorbed by *Maxwell*.

Stearns, 1923

Frank B. Stearns built a car in 1896, set up a factory in 1899, and left it in 1919. The make used the Knight sleeve-valve, was taken over by *Willys* in 1925 and called the *Stearns-Knight*. It ended in 1929.

Simplex, 1910

From 1907 on, a 4-cyl. 50hp car of the Mercedes type. *Henry M. Crane* designed a 6-cyl. family car, 1915-17, called the Simplex (Crane model). Production ceased after World War I.

White, 1903
2-cyl. steam-car,
also quite popular in Europe.

White "40," 1907
double-acting twin-cyl. steam engine

The origin of this make is to be found in a sewing-machine factory established in 1866 by *Thomas H. White,* which made bicycles during the 1890s. The founder's three sons *Windsor T., Rollin H.,* and *Walter C. White* made a steam-car in 1901 and built up a substantial output which from 1910 also included gasoline automobiles. Production of passenger cars ceased in 1918 in favor of trucks.

Childe Harold Wills was one of Henry Ford's most gifted engineers, but broke with him in 1919 and in 1921 brought out one brilliantly designed *Wills-Sainte Claire,* named after Lake Ste. Claire in Michigan. The first model's V-8 engine was copied from the Hispano-Suiza aero-engine. Later came the 6-cyl. "Gray Goose Traveller." The firm failed in 1927.

Wills-Sainte Claire, 1926
6-cyl. 82.55 × 139.7 mm,
4500 cc (3¼" × 5½", 274 cu.in.)

Willys-Knight, 1925
6-cyl. Knight sleeve-valve motor
82.55 × 120.65 mm, 3900 cc (3¼" × 4¾", 236 cu.in.)

Overland, 1926

The *Standard Wheel Co.* launched their *Overland* "buggy" in 1902. The model was not a success, although when a dealer, *John North Willys,* in desperation took over the *Overland Co.* in 1908 production methods were set to rights. The *Willys-Overland* company was formed, and in 1910 acquired the license to build Knight sleeve-valve motors which were used until 1933.

Stearns-Knight "8-90," 1928
Willys-Overland's 8-cyl. offering
in the higher price range.

Willys-Overland,
1939
4-cyl. 79.4×111.1 mm, 2200 cc (3⅛″×4⅜″, 134 cu.in.)

"Jeep Surrey," 1959

The robust side-valve 1925 *Overland* "whippet" engine proved so dependable that it was fitted to the war-time *Jeep,* still made today for more peaceful purposes. Car production stopped, apart from this, in 1954.

The Scottish immigrant *Alexander Winton* had had sound technical training, and took up the manufacture of cycle parts in 1890. His first car appeared in 1896, and one was sold in 1898. He raced with the "Bullet" models of 1902 and 1903.

Winton, 1900

In February 1946 *Preston Tucker* promised a car-hungry world a revolutionary rear-engined model with every conceivable refinement, at a price of $1000. The Tucker "Torpedo" was announced with loud fanfares of publicity —but the dream faded and only 49 were made before the Tucker joined the ranks of the vanished makes.

Winton, 1915

The factory kept such high standards that in 1924 it switched to marine diesels rather than build an inferior car.

Tucker "Torpedo" 1947

Grand Prix de l'Automobile Club de France, 1906

The motorcar had hardly made its appearance before man's eternal competitive urge had led to comparative tests, which soon turned into races. Open competition was the only means of deciding which car was the best, and since speed was the decisive feature for a means of transport, intrepid drivers raced their cars down the long roads of France.

Their sporting exploits were of inestimable value to technical development, and the competitors in races like the Paris-Bordeaux-Paris in 1895 and the races between Paris and other French cities which followed, the international events like Paris-Amsterdam-Paris and Paris-Berlin, hill-climbs, the Gordon Bennett matches, and other classics, enjoyed a reputation on a par with that of the first astronauts of the present day.

The races along the public roads of Europe came to a tragic end during the Paris-Madrid race of 1903. The French government put a stop to the race at the end of the first stage at Bordeaux, as there had been too many casualties among the public and the competitors. *Fernand Gabriel,* who had covered the 342 miles to Bordeaux in 5 hours (average 65.3 mph) was declared the winner after one of the most impressive feats of human endeavor in the annals of motor sport.

Races were now staged over closed circuits, and strict technical limitations were imposed on the cars in an attempt to insure that developments would be more in line with everyday needs.

The *Grand Prix de l'Automobile Club de France* rapidly became one of the most important international closed-circuit events. It was first held in 1906 over a distance of 769.9 miles, in two stages on consecutive days, and was won by *François Szisz* in a Renault. The following year the race was won by the Italian driver *Felice Nazzaro* in a *Fiat,* and in 1908 the German *Christian Lautenschlager* won for Mercedes. Competition had become truly international, and the financial stakes were high for participating manufacturers. The important races were few in number, and victory meant both a technical triumph and a substantial commercial profit.

◀ **Paris-Madrid,** 1903: *Gabriel's Mors*

Peugeot, 1913 GP model, driven by *Georges Boillot* in the Mont Ventoux hill-climb

In order to encourage the design of small cars rather than the giants previously in fashion, the journal *L'Auto* arranged a race in 1905 for light cars, the *Coupe des Voiturettes*. Both the nature of the race and its regulations changed between 1905-13, and loopholes in the regulations gradually led to such monstrous single-cylinder cars that Peugeot's works drivers *Georges Boillot, Paul Zuccarelli,* and *Jules Goux* began to think hard about the design of more civilized machines. Their ideas were put into practice in models designed by the Swiss engineer *Ernest Henry* in 1912. These incorporated—for the first time in one design —inclined overhead valves (four per cylinder), hemispherical combustion chambers, and twin overhead camshafts (p. 27). The larger of the two models won the 1912 French GP, and in 1913 the first place was again won with a 4-cyl. 5650 cc model (100×180 mm; 4″×7⅛″, 344.5 cu.in.). Georges Boillot, the driver of both cars, was hailed as the hero of French motor sport. In 1913 he drove Peugeot's GP model up the tortuous 13.4 miles of the Mont Ventoux hill-climb in 17 min. 38 sec. (46 mph), a record unbroken until 1925.

Monaco, 1929

The first *Grand Prix de Monaco* was run through the streets of Monte Carlo on April 14, 1929, when the Bugatti works driver *"Williams"* demonstrated the superior qualities of the "Type 35" on a difficult circuit. *Rudolf Caracciola* gained an astounding third place in the big *Mercedes-Benz*.

The *Grosser Preis von Deutschland* of 1935 did not appear to offer the Italians the slightest hope against the new German *Auto Union* and *Mercedes* cars; but it was won by *Tazio Nuvolari* in an *Alfa Romeo* after a fantastic drive.

Nürburgring, 1935

Montlhéry: a record-breaking **Jaguar "XK 120,"** August 1952

The first closed road circuits were so long that just keeping them closed and guarded was a major problem. This led to shorter courses, and a little later to special "autodromes" where cars could be extended to the limit of their performance. Both these solutions allowed the paying spectators to follow a race more easily than did the long road races in which the competitors passed the same spot only a very few times. The first specially built, permanent track was at *Brooklands* in England in 1907, followed by *Indianapolis* in the USA in 1909, *Monza* in Italy in 1922, *Montlhéry* in France in 1924, the *Nürburgring* in Germany in 1927, and several others in later years in the USA and elsewhere. The real autodromes with steeply banked corners have played an important part as test tracks for the car manufacturers, who are able to carry out high-speed trials undisturbed. These tracks are also the only places—apart from the salt flats at Utah— where record attempts can be made over long distances or periods. Brooklands very soon ceased really to count as a record circuit, partly because the local inhabitants had night driving prohibited and special silencers made compulsory, and partly because it proved bumpy and comparatively slow. Monza could be used in the periods between alterations, but Montlhéry was the Mecca of record-breakers for many years. Innumerable records have been set on its concrete oval. There are 4 categories of records in motor sport: *local* (on a given circuit), *national* (in a given country), *international class records* (best performance with a given motor size), and *world records* (best performance irrespective of motor size). Attempts are made in the individual categories over set times or distances. The regulations were laid down in 1904, and still apply, with a few changes in class limits, starting methods, etc. For Grand Prix racing at Montlhéry the closed road circuit and one half of the *"piste de vitesse"* have been used. In 1952 *Leslie Johnson, Stirling Moss, Jack Fairman,* and *Bert Hadley* drove a Jaguar "XK 120" for seven days and nights around the 1.6 miles of Montlhéry's oval track, covering 16,851.73 miles at 100.31 mph, and breaking 4 world records and 5 international class records in the process.

Brooklands, October 1935

Using a specially built *Napier-Railton, John R. Cobb* set an absolute record for the Brooklands Outer Circuit on October 7, 1935 at 143.44 mph. The track was not used after 1939, but during its 32 years of existence it provided a center for British motor racing and a marvelous venue for pensioned-off racing cars and outstanding special track models.

Grand Prix races are often run on artificial road circuits such as *Zandvoort* in Holland (*below*). The GP formula is framed by the FIA, the current regulations restricting engine-size to 1500 cc (91.46 cu.in.).

Le Mans: start, 1954

Sports car races were originally run with standard catalogue models. They still have the attraction of being, in theory, cars somewhat similar to everyday models. The 24-hour race at the *Sarthe* circuit at *Le Mans,* run since 1923, is one of the big annual events of the motor racing calendar. It provided a great show for the public, and an unrelenting struggle for the manufacturers taking part.

Special Frazer-Nash ("Patience")

◀ **Grote Prijs van Nederland,** 1961

The major international motor-sporting events are for professionals and the main considerations are commercial and technical; but these professionals are recruited from the amateur side of the sport, where the only limitations are the means, keenness, and ability of the competitors.

USA "board track," 1924

Road racing was abandoned early on in the USA, but was resumed after 1945. In the interim period races were run on earth or cinder tracks, the brick-paved track at Indianapolis, and, from 1910-30, a score of *board-tracks*. These perfectly smooth wooden tracks, hardly larger than bicycle stadiums, had corners so steeply banked that some permitted speeds of over 125 mph. Indianapolis continues a tradition of its own, with highly specialized cars.

Indianapolis

Daytona Beach 1935; *Sir Malcolm Campbell,* 276.82 mph

The world record for car speed was last set on a track (Brooklands) in 1922. When speeds approached 150 mph, record attempts were moved to stretches of shore. *Daytona Beach* in Florida was used from 1927-35 (and 1905-11). Since then ultra-high speed records have been set on *Bonneville Salt Flats,* Utah. The present record was set by John Cobb, who lost his life during a water speed record attempt.

Bonneville Salt Flats 1947; *John Rhodes Cobb,* 394.2 mph

INDEX

The names of marques are printed in **bold type** and those of designers, etc., are printed in *italics*.